Chesham
At Work
in the
20th Century

Keith Fletcher, Peter Hawkes & Lesley Perry

'Those who cannot remember the past are condemned to fulfil it'
George Santayana, Professor of Philosophy, Harvard University

'The further back you look, the further forward you can see'
Winston Churchill

First published in 2008 by Hawkes Design & Publishing Ltd

Copyright © 2008 Hawkes Design & Publishing Ltd

ISBN: 978-0-9554707-2-1

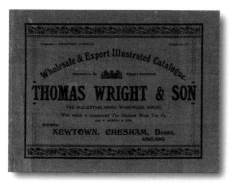

Contents

Foreword

Chesham is a great place in which to work. Writing as the Chairman of the Chesham Chamber of Trade & Commerce, I am pleased to say that we have over 100 business members who believe that Chesham is a thriving and enterprising community. The Chesham Chamber was founded in 1949, the first President being H W Carsberg, in a town that has a long history of commerce and industry, having offered employment across a broad range of industry sectors.

Chesham today has a strong retail and service sector and its location at the end of the Metropolitan Line provides businesses with the ideal of a rural market town situation with fast access to London. The business community is involved in networking, social and charitable activities, with a number of events throughout the year. Local retailers and the Chesham Chamber of Commerce are together responsible for the Victorian Evening, held on the last Friday of November each year, which celebrates Chesham's heritage. The success of the Chamber of Commerce and these associated activities is attributed to a positive and active local community supported by a dynamic Town Council.

Chesham at Work provides a unique insight into the history and culture of our market town.

Daniel Gregor
Chairman, Chesham Chamber of Trade & Commerce
October 2008

Introduction

The town of Chesham has been described as 'sleepy hollow,' and even today from the distant hills that surround the town, it presents a scene of quiet, rural beauty. However, it has always been a hub of industrious activity and its people known for their independence, non-conformity and uncanny willingness to work hard and turn their hands to many different jobs.

The industrial revolution led to a great change in the working life of Chesham folk in the mid-19th century. At the north end of the valley, the Newtown area developed to accommodate factories producing wooden ware, brushes and boots alongside which were built rows of terraced cottages to house the artisan workers. Small-scale wood turning was superseded by wooden ware manufacturing at the steam sawmills and factory workshops. Local specialities were wooden barn shovels, malt shovels, yokes, children's hoops and toys, butter prints and moulds, bread boards, spoons and bowls.

The off-cuts from wood turning had always been put to good use in the making of other useful items, including brush backs. In the 19th century, brush-making developed into a flourishing industry in Chesham, with mass production of fine quality products.

Footwear was another craft to be mechanised, with factories specialising in the output of heavy work boots – cut, sewn and riveted with the aid of machinery.

Further industrialisation, along with the coming of the railway in 1889, meant that the town saw mass employment and a rapidly expanding population as the 20th century commenced. Other traditional industries such as watercress growing and duck breeding benefited greatly from the improved transport system and, as more industries moved in, the town enjoyed a period of great self-sufficiency.

Many of the factory owners became pillars of the community, some serving on the Urban District Council. Some of these men built fine houses, such as Broadlands and Glenthorne, both now sadly long since demolished. The employers were fair-minded men, offering good wages and conditions. In return, employees were loyal and many spent their entire working life, from the age of 14, at one factory. Annual outings were organised for the workforce, to the seaside or to local beauty spots such as Burnham Beeches or Windsor Great Park. Originally by wagonette, by the 1920s they were by motor charabanc. By the 1930s the factories were providing paid holidays, most of them closing for the last week in July and the first week in August. The weekly wage at this time for a factory worker was about £2.

The invention of plastic and other new synthetic materials had a huge impact on Chesham's traditional industries, as did the increasing use of mechanisation. By mid century these industries were in decline but were rapidly replaced by new diverse ones. Many companies decided to move here because of the workers' reputation for industriousness, dexterity, loyalty and adaptability.

The Second World War also brought a variety of work and a number of businesses to the town. Forced out of London by the bombing, several companies relocated here to be within easy reach of the city.

This book attempts to document the history of the major companies that provided work and a livelihood for Cheshamites through the 20th century and to describe some of the many varied items that were produced in the town.

Below: View of Chesham from Marvel Hill, below Dungrove Farm (RE)

Aerial view of Chesham from the Broadway to Newtown, in 1928

1   Reynolds boot factory

2   First Co-op central premises

3   The Carlton Press

4   Brandon's department store

5   Wallis' blacksmiths

6   Charles Long's boot factory

7   Station goods yard

8   Chesham Brewery

9   James East's wood yard

10 Webb & Foulger brush works

11 Beechwood's brush factory

12 Giffard Newton boot factory

13 Racklyeft's boot factory

14 Chesham electricity power station

15 Tutill's flagmakers

16 Frederick East's wood yard

17 Thomas Wright's wood yard

18 Shillaker's handbag factory

19 Britannia boot and shoe factory

20 The Co-op boot and shoe factory

21 E Long & Sons' boot factory

22 Marie Antoinette hosiery factory

23 Hawes

24 Sundts

Chapter 1
Boots and shoes

Shoe making had been a major cottage industry in Chesham since the Middle Ages. By the 18th century, the town had two main tanneries, one in Water Lane next to a bark mill operated by William Mead, whose home was The Meades in Germain Street. The other tannery was in the High Street and belonged to the Hepburn family. Their imposing Georgian house still stands today, near the entrance to Sainsbury's. At that time the River Chess flowed nearby, before it was culverted beneath the High Street.

The tanneries required three main elements – hides, water and tannin. Hides came from local slaughterhouses, water for cleaning them from the river and tannin from tree bark, ground in the mill. The town became one of the main centres for shoe production for the London market. During the 19th century, shoemakers were producing the heavy boots worn by most working men. This was practical for a variety of occupations, being of durable leather, with steel toe-caps and soles studded with hob nails. According to the census of 1851, there were 291 male shoemakers and 85 female shoe binders in the town. Small craft workshops continued, but with only a few men, and by late in the century several factories were built, mostly in the developing Newtown area. In the 1896 *Kelly's Commercial Directory* there were 16 boot and shoe manufacturers in Chesham and several other businesses listed as 'boot and shoe makers, warehouses and dealers'.

Gradually machinery took the place of the hand craftsman and workers specialised as 'clickers,' 'closers' and 'riveters' (see glossary below). The term 'clicker' may come from the sound made in the process. Employers 'rose from the ranks' and could perform every process of manufacture themselves. Some of the products were sold locally in the boot and shoe shops, but the majority were taken by horse and cart to the station, to be despatched to London and beyond.

During the 20th century the industry steadily declined, as more and more working people came to favour the wearing of shoes rather than the heavy boot. Many of the Chesham factories failed to adapt to this change in fashion and today there is only one business remaining in the trade, Giffard Newton, which is no longer a manufacturer.

Glossary of boot/shoe making terms

tannery – the place where animal hides are turned into leather

currier – person who dresses the tanned hide to make it strong, flexible and waterproof

uppers – the upper part of a boot or shoe

clicker – person who cuts out and shapes the uppers

closer – person, often female, who sews and stiffens the uppers

riveter – person, usually male, who attaches the sole to the upper

hob nails – large head nails driven into the soles for grip/wear

straights – boots that could be worn on either foot

butts – bundles of animal hides

grindery – leather-workers' tools and materials

anklejack – name given to early navvy boots

Blake machine *(pictured)* – a chain stitch machine for fastening the sole to the shoe. Its large size forced manufacture into factories *(courtesy British United Shoe Machinery)*

last – a wooden/metal foot shape around which leather is formed

Small workshops

In the early years of the century there were a few small workshop manufacturers still operating.

James Butterfield, 59 Waterside;

Darvell & Jennings, later **Henry Joseph Jennings** in Bellingdon Road (later Atlas Pencil Co, now Atlas House);

Joseph How, 250 Berkhampstead Road;

Stephen Henry Quelch & Co and **Percy James Taylor & Co,** Berkhampstead Road;

The Chesham Manufacturing Co, Progressive Works, Townsend Road. Listed *Kelly's Directory* 1907. Probable precursor to the Chesham Boot & Shoe Manufacturers Ltd of Higham Road.

W V Butler Ltd, Severalls Avenue and **J H Woodington** in Alma Road (both early 1930s);

George Wheeler, Berkhampstead Road;

R G Poole, Broad Street

Reynolds boot factory staff, Blucher Street, c1910 (RE)

Joseph Glasgow had a factory in Townsend Road from the 1870s. A serious fire on 15 August 1905 caused the roof and upper floor to collapse, although the walls remained intact. The lower floors were damaged only by smoke, water and falling debris. Books and the contents of the glass office were undamaged. There was considerable financial loss as the business was only partially covered by insurance. The most valuable leather stock had been stored in the upper floors and this was totally destroyed. The contents of the machine room were burnt out and the riveters' workshop suffered a great deal of damage from heat, smoke and water. The factory does not appear in subsequent issues of the *Kelly's Directory* so was presumably not rebuilt.

James and Edwin Reynolds started a boot and shoe manufacturing business in the High Street in the late 1860s. By 1877 they were advertising themselves as wholesale and export boot and shoe manufacturers in Blucher Street and curriers, grindery dealers and leather merchants in Market Square. In the 1881 census James was 45, unmarried, employing 81 men, 21 boys and 15 women and living in Bury Hill End with his widowed mother and unmarried younger sister. His younger brother Edwin was listed as a boot maker and living in Market Square with his wife and young family.

An article in the *Bucks Examiner* in 1889 describes a tour of the factory. Visible were a variety of hides – natural brown for Army boots, delivered unblacked; black skins for navvies' anklejacks; calf skins for police boots and waterproof German horse hides. In the clicking department, skins were laid on wooden blocks and a zinc pattern was cut around using a sharp knife. In the heavy machine room, uppers of stouter boots were 'closed'. A Whittimore machine was used for sewing, using waxed thread. 50 pairs per hour could be sewn and other machines attached the toe caps.

Soles were made from imported leather from South America, arriving in 'butts' or bundles of skins. Singapore leather was used

for the inner casing. Tough and close-textured butts were sliced into long strips and the contour of the sole roughly outlined. Three tons of pressure was then applied with a machine which stamped out the exact form required. A Blake machine was used for stitching the soles in around 24 seconds. This would have taken up to 45 minutes by hand. Another machine consolidated the thicknesses of leather forming the soles while yet another performed the riveting. In the fitting room, nails and tips were applied as required, then a paring machine smoothed the edges. In the girls' room, where the closing of lighter boots was carried out, there were about a dozen machines. These were for sewing seams, making buttonholes or embroidering patterns on patent leather. There was a Bradbury Repairer for patching boots needing repair.

The Reynolds brothers' Oak Tree Boot and Shoe Co in Market Square (RE)

In the making-up department, all the work was done by hand. About 70 workmen riveted boots on a last or applied wooden pegs for shipboard boots, as no iron was permitted.

By 1891 the brothers were also 'contractors to the British and Foreign governments' and were producing around 2,000 pairs of boots per week. James was now living in Blucher Street, but Edwin had built himself a grand mansion, Broadlands, in White Hill. It had a long driveway from the road and the house and drive are now commemorated as Broadlands Avenue. Edwin was the first Chairman of the Chesham Urban District Council in 1894.

In addition, by 1899 the brothers had a boot and shoe warehouse, the **Oak Tree Boot and Shoe Co**, in Market Square *(pictured previous page)*. It operated until around 1925, selling a wide range of footwear including ladies' lightweight shoes. Prices varied from 1s 6d to 4s 11d for a pair of shoes, to 6s 11d for heavy boots. They also carried out repairs.

E Long & Sons were in Sunnyside Road in the early years of the century. The business had been started by Charles Long, son of shoemaker Charles, of Germain Street. In 1881, at the age of 28, Charles Jr was a boot and shoe manufacturer living in Newtown, with a young family. His younger brother John, 25, was a shoe manufacturer at 44 Church Street, employing 18 men, two women and three boys. By 1889 Charles was so successful he had opened a new showroom and offices at 79 High Street. With the coming of the Metropolitan Railway that year, many customers preferred to visit the showroom rather than to choose from a list or samples. Charles already had the second largest boot factory in town after Reynolds and also ran an extensive leather and grindery goods business. There were around 80 employees. At this time he was specialising in 'nailed and strong plain goods' – navvies' 'watertights'; ploughmen's 'keepers'; carters' boots and shooting boots, but 'no lighter fancy boots'. He felt these were not appropriate for Chesham and its conditions. He was producing 1,000 pairs of boots each week and demand was such that he expected to increase to 1,200 pairs, but needed to look for larger premises. The intention was that the town centre premises would be used for warehousing and storage. There was no extensive use of machinery yet, unlike the Reynolds' factory, but it was expected that some would be installed in the new factory. In 1891 his eldest son, 16-year-old Herbert, was an assistant in the business. Charles had nine other children by this time and was employing a general servant and a nursemaid at the family home, 140 Bellingdon Road.

A fire in May 1905 was reported as being at F Long's Sunnyside Road factory. The wooden building was gutted and machinery and stock were completely destroyed. Fortunately the business was insured but it had only been a few months since Frederick, Charles'

A view inside the factories

Finishing room, c1900, Britannia Works (RE)

Clicking room, c1920, Britannia Works (RE)

Workers with lasts at Barnes & Son (RB)

second son, had rented the premises from Messrs Abbott, after carrying out the necessary alterations. It had previously been occupied by Abel Mead & Burton, builders. Valuable machinery had been installed and 30 to 40 hands engaged. An electrical fault had been detected a few weeks previously, the factory was closed while the defect was remedied, so there were no employees present when fire broke out at the back of the building. After the fire Charles Long set his sons up in farming, and Frederick went out to Sweetwater, Montana in the United States (he later returned to East Sussex where he died in 1963).

By 1907 the business appeared in *Kelly's Directory* under E Long & Sons at a factory in Sunnyside Road. E Long is believed to be Charles' wife, Elizabeth. A brochure from this time assures the purchaser of the quality of the products, stressing the durability, reliability, but cheap prices of the boots and shoes and the special attention given to the inner soles. All classes of boots and shoes were made to measure, hand sewn, machine sewn or riveted. Repairs could also be carried out.

'The healthiest people and the longest-lived people are those who wear good boots. Therefore look well to your feet, and if you wish to live long, and be healthy and happy, wear Long's boots', proclaimed their brochure. However, the company appears to have finished by 1928. Its downfall was most likely because it continued to stress the importance of strong work boots and did not adapt to the lighter shoes coming into vogue.

John Hayes & Sons operated from a factory at 71-79 Waterside, built c1890. His father James had been a boot and shoe maker in Waterside from around 1850. John gradually built up his business over the years and his sons William John and Ernest later joined him as partners. John Edward Randall (father of well-known local teacher Jim Randall) worked his way up to factory foreman. John Hayes and his family lived at The Thorns, a house behind the factory fronting onto Amersham Road. His sons continued the business after his death, into the early 1930s, until this business too succumbed to a slump in demand for their speciality heavy boots.

Mitchell's boot factory workers outside their Church Street premises (RE)

Thomas Mitchell

Thomas Mitchell ran a boot and shoe business at 46-48 Church Street from the late 19th century. This is one of the oldest buildings in Chesham, dating from the 15th century. He lived upstairs, above the ground floor workshop. Through the yard at the side of the building to the rear was the old tanning pit. This yard was named after Thomas when it became Mitchell's Yard. Thomas worked originally in the wooden ware industry, possibly William Wright's sawmill in Water Lane and may then have worked at David Newton's boot factory in Church Street.

He was clearly a very competent and motivated young man because in 1875, at the age of only 23, he was the prime mover in setting up the Chesham Co-operative Society. He fulfilled many roles for the Society in his spare time, including secretary, treasurer, buyer and canvasser. His son Thomas Jr joined him in the business, which continued into the 1950s.

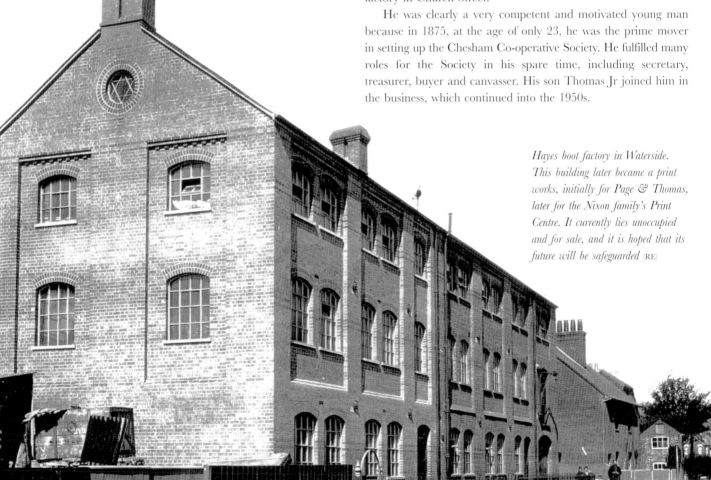

Hayes boot factory in Waterside. This building later became a print works, initially for Page & Thomas, later for the Nixon family's Print Centre. It currently lies unoccupied and for sale, and it is hoped that its future will be safeguarded (RE)

The British United Shoe Machinery Co Ltd was a Leicester-based company with several depots throughout England, including one in Chesham, at 58 Townsend Road. This emphasises the importance of boot and shoe making in the town, as depots were established in every shoe-making centre in the country. Their purpose was to support the boot manufacturers by providing machines and accessories and supplying advice on setting up new factories or modernising old ones.

The setting up of BUSM originated with the creation of the United Shoe Machinery Company in the United States in February 1899. This was an amalgamation of several engineering companies, each of which specialised in the manufacture of particular types of footwear machinery. The combined company was the only one able to supply a footwear manufacturer with all his machinery needs and in the

Depot at 58 Townsend Road,
(Illustration courtesy of BUSM)

first few years of its existence it acquired many other smaller businesses. BUSM was formed in October 1899 by an amalgamation of the English branches of the American companies which formed USM, together with a Leicester engineering concern, Pearson and Bennion Ltd, which manufactured shoe machinery.

In later years all the machinery was manufactured at the Leicester factory and it became the world's largest manufacturer of machinery and materials for the footwear industry. In its 1970s heyday, BUSM was the city's biggest employer, with a workforce of more than 4,500 exporting shoe machinery to more than 50 countries around the world. In 1990 it won a Queen's Award for Export. In 2000 the company went into receivership and was wound up in 2003. The Chesham depot had ceased operating in the 1950s when it was incorporated into the London one.

Frederick Racklyeft started a business in Higham Road in the early 1900s. Like the other boot factories, they had to supply army boots during the two world wars. It is thought there were around 20 employees. When Frederick died in 1922 the business was continued by his youngest son, Henry, until his death in 1943. It was then taken over by Henry's son Ewart until 1952, when he ceased trading, retired and sold the factory to Golden Ltd (cosmetics and hair dyes). Ewart's cousin Bill, son of Frederick's son Fred, was also involved until the closure, when he went to work for Giffard Newton. The name Racklyeft is believed to be a corruption of Ratcliffe or Radcliffe, though it has been in existence in this form for some considerable time.

He went on to found his own business from humble beginnings, making boots in the front room of his own home. In 1884 he started a small business in Church Street, later moving to the High street. Several members of the Barnes family were involved in boot or shoe making. In 1891 George and his brother John had a shoe manufactory in Severalls Avenue. In 1894 George was elected to the Chesham Urban Council. He lived at Britannia Villas in Berkhampstead Road initially, having built this pair of houses in the late 1880s but in the 1920s he moved to Broadlands, the large mansion in White Hill built by Edwin Reynolds. (This was demolished in the early 1950s).

In 1899 George built one of the first factories on what was then the outskirts of the town, in Addison Road and known as the **Britannia Boot & Shoe Works.** This caused some criticism, as it was felt that he would not find sufficient workers willing to travel so far. However, the business built up quickly and became very successful. The factory was constructed of brick and the most up-to-date quality machinery was installed.

In the early days, work boots of all kinds were the speciality, including 'straights' – boots that could be worn on either foot. Boots for hill farmers and shepherds were made, turned up at the toe for better grip on hills and steep inclines. Soles were leather and patterned with hob nails. Skilled workers could hold up to 12 nails in their mouths, removing them one at a time to hammer into the leather and create fancy designs. Workers were on 'piece work', paid for the number of boots they made during their 48-hour week. 'Tubby' Reading was a familiar sight each weekday when he carted crates of boots to the station for transporting all over Britain and Ireland.

The interior of the Britannia factory extension, 1920s (RB)

With the outbreak of the First World War, the army needed an endless supply of boots and Barnes was one of many factories who produced them, although Northampton provided the majority. After the war he went to America as one of a deputation from the Boot and Shoe Manufacturers' Federation, to inspect the American factories. In the early 1920s George's sons George Jr and Maurice took over the running of the business. At some point an extension had been added to the original building and around this time another, separate single-storey building was constructed on the other side of the yard, later joined to the original factory by a bridge. This became the main manufacturing area. The second floor of the original building was then used for the storage and cutting of the leather.

Several of the old factories of the traditional industries had sports teams and some of the employees were keen footballers

A branch of the **Webb** family was involved from the early 19th century in the shoe and boot industry, in Waterside. Joseph Webb had a business in the High Street in the latter years of the century. At one time **George Barnes** worked for him.

Above: the office at Britannia works, with the framed photo on the wall, as shown left

playing for Chesham Generals or Chesham United. In 1924, Maurice Barnes was tragically killed in an accident whilst playing for Chesham United. He usually played in the reserves but on this occasion he was replacing someone. Another player, later trainer, Harry Bates, worked for Barnes all his life.

George Sr died in 1933 and there was a huge turnout for his funeral and interment at Chesham Cemetery, in the same grave as his son Maurice. The coffin was carried by six long-serving employees. He had been a much-respected employer and member of the community. He was a keen sportsman, captaining the county bowls team and interested in many other sports, particularly while his sons George Jr and Maurice were involved with Chesham United. He was a generous supporter of many good causes and belonged to both the Freemasons and the Order of Oddfellows. He was at one time Chairman of the Urban Council. George's son Robert (Bob) and son-in-law Dick Goodson (well-known in 1935 as the British bowls champion and who lived in one half of Britannia Villas), joined George Jr in the running of the business.

Up to 2,000 pairs of heavy boots were being produced each week; some of the female workers left to work on softer leather in nearby Shillaker's handbag factory, opened in the 1920s. During the Second World War army boots were again in demand. This time the Government required that 60-70 percent of boot manufacturing output had to be for the army. Government inspectors checked every pair of boots for quality before they were stamped Ministry of Defence. Steel toe caps began to be produced because of George's friendship with George Denton, whom he had met at London meetings of the Boot and Shoe Manufacturers' Federation. Denton had introduced them from the United States in the late 1930s and the Government were insisting on better Health and Safety standards. Barnes began to supply large retailers, heavy industry and the building trade.

In the late 1950s George was diagnosed with a terminal illness and his sons Richard, John and David moved into the business as they left school. A school friend, Barrie Lucke, joined them and eventually became a director. By the 1960s vulcanisation had been developed, a process whereby rubber soles could be bonded with adhesives to the leather upper. This proved difficult for many factories, who could not afford investment in new machinery; others were not inclined to do so. Both the Chesham Boot & Shoe Manufacturing Co and Frederick Racklyeft's business closed at this time. Bill Racklyeft, one of Frederick's sons, joined Giffard Newton and Tom Clark from the CBSM Co came to Barnes.

On a cold January morning in 1968 a serious fire broke out at the factory. Much of the roof was destroyed and the upper floor collapsed but the rest of the building survived. The Fire Brigade were hampered by the intense cold as the steep incline of Addison Road quickly became a sheet of ice and water from the hoses froze. Employees were paid in full while the factory was rebuilt.

In the mid-1960s Barnes received an order worth £80-90,000 from the Coal Board for 15,000 pairs of steel toe-capped boots for miners at collieries nationwide. However, it proved increasingly difficult for Chesham's two remaining boot factories to survive, making the same product and chasing the same orders. Finally, in 1980 it was agreed that Barnes would merge with Giffard Newton & Sons Ltd. Some specialist orders were for non-conductive and anti-

Business meeting at Northampton, c1955: l to r: Frank Brown, George Denton, Dick Goodson, Bob Barnes, George Barnes.

(All photos this page courtesy of Richard Barnes)

George Barnes & Co, c1935. Two men are wearing their 'breast leathers' – laced on to protect clothing from the wear of bench and boots (RB)

static boots for ICI, for employees working near electric circuits and wires. The Britannia works was sold in 1983 to Sensonics and in 1988 it was gradually demolished and a new double-glazed factory with 18,000 square feet of accommodation was erected behind it.

In 1895 a co-operative productive society began in Chesham, mainly making army boots but this was short lived. However, a similar organisation re-emerged as the **Chesham Boot and Shoe Manufacturers Ltd** following a meeting of boot workers held in March 1900. After a further series of discussions they decided to start their own boot factory, raising the money themselves from their own subscriptions and meagre savings and 'taking the future in their hands'. Two years later they registered as a Productive Society, the first fund being known as the Equity Production Fund.

Their original premises were in a hay-loft behind the Chesham Co-operative shop in Blucher Street. In 1904 they were ready to start production. Samples were shown to the committee and they were priced before being taken out 'on the road'; this was mostly to Co-operative Societies. Later in the year a stall was taken at the Congress Exhibition in Stratford, where a big Co-operative Society had been established. The first manager, Mr G L Hollis *(pictured)*, was appointed; he also acted as traveller.

A workshop was rented in Sunnyside Road, belonging to Mr C Catling. The first Minutes recorded 'the future looks good' but it was a long hard journey to success. The first accounts, in an exercise book, mentioned weekly sums of three shillings paid out to part-time workers. That first year showed a loss and there were no reserves to fall back on. However, the members found the money to continue themselves and by 1907 they were able to move to a new building in Higham Road. They gradually increased in staff and production and made a place for themselves in the production of the heavy boots for which Chesham was known. They survived until 1959 with many of the original workers or committee members. These included footballer Charles Wingfield, Fred Goodger, John Davis and Frank Mayger, who worked full-time at the factory for 42 years.

Mr Hollis went on to hold a secretarial and management position with Chesham Co-operative Society and was a noted local singer. Fred Goodger was a footballer and cricketer who later became a Trade Union secretary. Of other workers, W V Butler

went on to found his own boot factory. George Payne, originally a boot riveter, was a founder member who was secretary until 1934. His wife Kate would take him a can of tea and, whilst there, was often given a brush and a pot of dye to colour the edges of the cut-out shapes of leather.

Giffard Newton is the last survivor of Chesham's long history of boot and shoe making. As with the Barnes family, there were several Newtons involved in boot and shoe making. In 1881 brothers Frederick, Henry, David, George and Edwin either had their own businesses or were working in the trade in some capacity. George was a boot clicker and Edwin a leather cutter, whilst the others were manufacturers, David employing three men in Church Street and Henry employing 12 men in Red Lion Street.

David Newton supplied the Irish navvies building the A40 with the strong waterproof boots called 'anklejacks'. These supported the foot and particularly the ankle, protecting it from the dangers of laying roads on heavy stone foundations. He also produced boots for farm workers, hob nailed for gripping wet muddy fields when following the plough. The demand for these gradually declined with the introduction of the tractor. Originally agricultural footwear was known by the trade name 'Landking'. A spring-toed last was developed to make shepherds' boots, with a flexible sole at the toe end for ease of walking on the hills. 'Straights' were produced, which could be worn on either foot. There was great demand for these as they could be changed around, ensuring even wear on both sides, prolonging their life. Left and right boots were also produced, however, as some men preferred them.

David Newton died in 1891, leaving his three sons to manage the business. The youngest son, Harvey, continued the parent company until he died in the 1920s. By 1915 the older sons George and Robert had built a new factory of their own in Townsend Road, with a family home at the front of the factory, facing the road. This was later demolished as the factory expanded. They produced a variety of heavy boots for manual workers at home and abroad. The Ministry of Defence dictated output during the two World Wars and supplied materials for army boots. During the Second World War, boots were inspected for quality before being stamped for acceptance. No profits were made during this time and no money was made available for maintenance of equipment and machinery. American boots were less durable than British ones and Newtons' repaired many of them. The quality was so superior that GIs continued to acquire British boots after they had returned home. Giffard Newton and his sons were running the business by 1933 as a private limited company.

Church Street factory used by Newton's at one time

Newtons' boot workers, 1930s (RE)

Boots and shoes with internal steel toe caps were made to meet European standards for people working in a variety of hazardous occupations. They protected the feet in case of a heavy weight falling on the toes. Thick leather soles ensured that nails and sharp objects could not penetrate.

In the 1950s a direct vulcanising machine was developed, enabling rubber to be moulded onto the leather uppers. This process was invented by CIC Ralph's, part of the Clarks Shoes group. The soles could be automatically applied, of polyurethane. They were acid and oil resistant to a temperature of 300°C. Around 5,000 pairs were made each week, sometimes as many as 6,000. They were very hard-wearing with a life of about 20 years. They had the brand name Tuffking, coined by Giffard Newton Jr *(pictured right)*, grandson of David. He had joined the firm at the age of 19 and worked from 7.30am to 6pm for £1 per week. A new company was formed, **Tuffking Safety Ltd**, in Broad Street, managing director George Banfield. J Tuffney was the Senior Foreman at Newtons' and became one of the leading experts in the country on moulded shoes.

In 1957 Newtons' made a pair of boots for Dirk Bogarde when he appeared in the film version of *A Tale of Two Cities*, filmed at Pinewood Studios. The boots were built up to make him appear taller. In 1969 a new piece of equipment was installed which made the workers' lives easier and quieter. It was a conveyor belt system known as the Duo-Rail Transporter and it was expected that a 30 percent increase in production would be the result. The machine was almost silent in operation and gave the firm a lot more space. Workers were placed at intervals along the belt and each man could adjust its speed to suit his own rate of work. At that time demand was high and the business was planning to expand.

In 1976 and 1977 Newtons' had a contract with the National Coal Board to produce Chukka boots for surface workers at the collieries. 8,000 pairs were supplied in 1977, an order worth £40,000. In the late 1970s, sturdy high-class walking boots were introduced into the range. Up until then the market had been dominated by imports. It was beneficial to the company to produce them at the factory, as there was always a slump in safety boots during the summer months. 'High Country' was the brand name and £500,000 worth was produced during March to September each year. They were available through specialist camping shops, were also exported to Norway, Belgium, France and the Middle East and were successful for about 20 years. However, by then cheaper imports from the Far East were available and so it was decided to concentrate on firemen's boots instead.

The company merged with George Barnes & Sons Ltd in the 1980s (see earlier entry). In 1983 it supplied the BBC with polar boots for their documentary on Shackleton's Antarctic Expedition. Around 1985 Newton's became the first company to produce leather firemen's boots. Previously they wore rubber wellington boots, which were

The 'Beva' boot brand, another of Giffard Newton's lines (CN)

heavy and uncomfortable. The new leather boots were lighter, waterproof and breathable and conformed to European standards. Thousands were produced and exported – well over 2,000 pairs per week. The company has now been the market leader in the UK for firemen's boots for around 40 years. Employees numbered around 95 at the peak of production in the late 1970s, about one-third of whom were women. They were all from the town and were very loyal to the company, two or three generations of the same family often working at the factory. Salaries were comparable to other factories in Chesham.

Around 5 million pairs of safety footwear were sold per year in the UK, with three percent imported. By the end of the 1990s that statistic had risen to 98 percent. Domestic cows had been originally used for the leather, the major tanneries being in Liverpool and Hull. Gradually cheaper leather was imported, for example water buffalo from India, and by the late 1990s the complete product was being manufactured in Kanpur in India. The company presently works with factories in India, but increasingly China is becoming a major producer, particularly with the current weakness of the dollar. However, these boots have to meet rigid European quality and safety standards.

In 1991 the First Gulf War broke out and Newtons' received an order for desert combat boots. Today the Ministry of Defence sources its supplies from an agency. Items can be ordered online from China, Korea, India or Pakistan. In 2007 there were 65,000 fire fighters in Britain and 45,000 of them were wearing Tuffking boots, including the London Fire Brigade and the Buckinghamshire brigades. Clive Newton took an interest in the company from childhood. On leaving school he studied for a business degree and then decided to join his father, Giffard Jr, in the family firm, becoming its last Director.

In 2005 the business was sold to MK Associates, a shoe company supplying High Street stores nationwide. The factory closed, the business was moved to an industrial unit in Higham Mead and warehousing transferred to Essex. Although they will retain the Giffard Newton name, the end of an era has been reached, as boots are no longer made in the town. However, the company is still involved in the design, import and distribution of safety footwear and fire boots.

Giffard Newton's at Townsend Road

Chapter 2
Brush-making

The brush-making industry developed from the vast quantities of offcuts of wood left over from shovel-making. These were used to form the brush backs. Originally a cottage industry, brushes were entirely made by hand. In the late 19th century factories opened up, machinery was gradually introduced and hand brush-making evolved into mass production, although certain quality brushes are still made by hand to this day at Russell Brothers (see page 23). In its heyday there were around a dozen factories producing every conceivable kind of brush from nailbrushes and the smallest paintbrushes to the largest brooms. Several specialist brushes were made, including ones for cleaning dairy equipment, or for lamp glasses. These were sent all over the country and exported to parts of Europe. Bristles were imported, usually from China. Nylon was later introduced and soon many factories were using this instead of natural bristle. Competition caused one factory after another to close down, until today only Russell Brothers remains.

Webb's was the oldest brush manufacturers in the town. Founded in 1829 by Robert Webb, formerly a wood turner with his father and grandfather, in a small yard in the Broadway (currently occupied by a large café) every process was originally performed by hand. Much of the work was carried out by workers in their own homes and the finished brushes returned. Brush backs were shaped from the local beech wood, holes in the brush stocks were drilled by hand and the bristles glued in individually. Bristle came from Russia and Poland in large casks, tied in bundles and had to be prepared. This involved 'dragging' into lengths, grading and cleaning. Local horsehair was also used in the early days, combings from manes and tails. This had to be cleaned, steamed and straightened before it could be used. Later Robert and his two sons, George and William, designed and built steam-driven machinery and were the

At the drying sheds (RE)

first brush manufacturers in the country to introduce mechanisation. Steam power meant coal had to be transported by road from Berkhamsted, a stop on the London and Birmingham railway line. Unfortunately, in 1864 there was a fire in which all the early records were lost. The factory was badly damaged but was soon rebuilt and in 1870 a further factory built alongside.

In 1878 a factory was built in Townsend Road to develop the mechanised side of the business and machines were built on these premises. In 1889 an automatic filling machine was built, claimed to be one of the first in the country. It was in daily use for over 30 years. In 1897 a much larger factory was built and the firm moved permanently from the Broadway to the Townsend Road site.

Webb's had become a major employer in the town, particularly of girls. Daughters of generations of lace makers and straw plaiters, they were well able to manage the delicate and intricate work involved in brush-making. At this time the business was known as R Webb & Sons Ltd, Steam Brush Works.

For nearly 100 years they produced brushes for all domestic and industrial cleaning purposes. These included brushes for such diverse purposes as road sweeping, for the dairy, for vacuum cleaners and for cleaning barnacles from ships' hulls.

Around the turn of the century George Webb, by now a JP, built a grand family home, Glenthorne, in Bellingdon Road. With seven bedrooms, fireplaces of Italian marble in the reception rooms and Italian tiles on the hall floor, it would have been one of the most impressive houses in Chesham at the time. There was stained glass in the windows on the landing, in the hall and in one of the bedrooms. A conservatory led off the breakfast room. The kitchen had a range to heat the water and there was some central heating. The house stood in its own landscaped grounds with a large lawn and trees including a copper beech and a weeping hornbeam.

With the outbreak of the First World War, Webb's lost many of its young men to war service. A young schoolboy called Fred Sabatini helped his family by working before and after school for 2s 6d (12½p) per week. After leaving school at 14 he joined the factory full-time and remained as such until he officially retired in 1970 but continued to work two mornings per week until 1980. He began by helping to sort out the fibre but finished as foreman. Interviewed for *Berks and Bucks Countryside* in 1980, he remembered

WEBB'S BRUSH MANUFACTORY,
BROADWAY, CHESHAM, BUCKS.

The rear of Webb's factory in the Broadway (RE)

Webb's Townsend Road interior – shaping and drilling shop (RE)

that on payday, every employee lined up to receive their pay packet from Harry Webb, grandson of the founder. Fred was so excited to receive his first pay packet, containing ten shillings, that he ripped open the envelope and threw it in the fire. On finding the envelope empty, he realised that his pay was a ten-shilling note and that was on the fire too. 'It took a long time to make up the money' he said.

Around 1919 the company merged with F Foulger & Co to become **Webb and Foulger Ltd** and began making paintbrushes for professional decorators. Later, brushes and rollers would also be produced for the expanding 'Do It Yourself' market. Domestic brushware was reduced, though brushes for industrial use were still produced.

In 1931 Wilfred Lawson Broad, a New Zealander by birth, joined the company as chief engineer. He went on to build machines and re-organise that side of the business with a great deal of success. One of the first things he did on joining the firm was to install electric lighting and power. His son Alex joined the firm after military service in 1953 and after training in various aspects of the trade he decided to work in the paint brush department.

In 1940 the directors were H G Webb and A E Webb, grandsons of Robert, Ronald W Webb, a great-grandson, and C S Holton, one of the founders of F Foulger & Co. A E Webb was at that time a vice-president of the British Brush Manufacturers' Association, which had been established in 1908.

Architects' drawing of Webb's, Townsend Road, 1905 (RE)

For many years the company concentrated on supplying other manufacturers and later an export trade was built up, particularly with Australia and New Zealand, until they established their own manufacturers. Trade with China was once important but became difficult under Communism. However, by the 1950s a considerable export trade was still being carried on with West Africa, the West Indies, Hong Kong and Malaya, amongst other countries.

A further merger occurred in 1948 with F Jarratt & Co of Huddersfield. Frank Jarratt, an engineer by training, had formed his company in 1931. Two small subsidiary companies were closed and Chesham became the headquarters, with a branch factory in Huddersfield. In 1954 the paintbrush department and timber mill were destroyed by fire. Within a week, work had resumed in three Nissen huts and a year later a new factory was in production. At some point Frank Jarratt was president of the British Brush Manufacturers' Association.

Always at the forefront of new developments, **Webb, Jarratt & Co Ltd** was among the first British brush companies to produce pure bristle brooms using a plastic-setting process. This ensured a quality sweeping product combined with a setting unaffected by heat or damp.

Advertisement in a 1940's brush brochure (ABR)

In 1959 the company, now employing around 120 people, became part of the United Transport Group. They were one of the leading producers of painting and sweeping brushware in the UK. In 1967 Mr Jarratt resigned as Managing Director of the Dendix Industrial Brush Group, to which Webb Jarratt had belonged since 1963. Mr A Dutton was at that time director and general manager, responsible for both the Chesham and the Huddersfield companies. At Christmas 1967 the company was able to announce

A brush machine ready for production, made in the engineering and machine repair shop. Wilfred Lawson Broad standing far right (RE)

its best ever sales figures, 'the result of steady progress over the past few years' according to Mr Dutton. There were by then 158 employees.

In early 1972 the company won a safety award from the British Safety Council. Its accident rate for the previous year had been lower than the national average for the brush-making industry. Then works manager Geoff Lawrence, who had joined the firm in 1936, said that the firm 'probably makes a greater effort than many companies, sending people on safety courses and making sure that none of the equipment in the factory is unsafe'. Award-winning companies were entitled to fly the green and white safety flag above their premises and were invited to send representatives to the Safety Council's annual banquet in London.

Webb Jarratt's, viewed from Albany Place in the 1980s (RE)

By the mid-1970s the Dendix group had taken over a German group, increasing sales throughout Europe. Webb Jarratt was already exporting specialised brushes to the Middle East, Far East and America, including street-cleaning equipment to Hong Kong. By the late 1970s it was a member of Brushes International.

Sadly the business finished in March 1983 owing to the changing economic climate and the strength of foreign competition. Production of many items including specialised brushes was transferred to Brushes International's other factories at Acton and Chepstow. The factory and three Victorian houses were demolished and a DIY retail warehouse, Great Mills, built with the opportunity of around 30 jobs. This later became a Focus store.

George **Hawes** started a brush-making business at 101 Bellingdon Road in the 1880s. His sons William George and Henry Whitmill continued, but were finished at this site by 1913 when the first Chiltern Toy works appeared here (see Toy section). Henry was working as a tailor in the High Street in 1915 but William George had started his own brush-making business in a three-storey building on the corner of Cameron Road at 217 Berkhampstead Road. There was a fire not long afterwards and the top floor was destroyed. The business continued after renovation, though with only two floors. They produced shoe brushes, clothes brushes, scrubbing brushes, brushes for black-leading kitchen ranges and brooms.

Damage after the fire at Hawes' factory on the corner of Cameron Road (RE)

There were some female employees who worked from home, hand-filling the already drilled brush stocks. Otherwise the work was done by machine in the factory. Brush backs were beech and the bristle came mainly from China. Brushes were packed into very large hampers and taken to London by train. William's three sons Reg, Horace and George all worked in the business and became directors after their father's death in 1939. William and his brother Henry had married two Cason sisters. William's sons Reg and George continued the tradition by marrying two Dean sisters. The factory closed in the early 1960s when George retired. The building is now known as Brae House and is occupied by offices. The Hawes at one time lived in a house at the top of White Hill, known as Brae Side.

In 1914 Robert Preston lived at 107 Bellingdon Road and also occupied 119-121 Bellingdon Road. By 1928 **Robert Preston & Co Ltd**, brush manufacturers, were at Nashleigh Hill and Robert lived next door. Preston Hill is named to commemorate him.

In 1891 **Lloyd Williams** was a brush maker in Berkhampstead Road. By 1899 he had moved to 106 Bellingdon Road and was there until at least 1928. So it seems that Beechwood Brushes probably absorbed several smaller businesses.

Beechwood Brushes Ltd in Bellingdon Road had its origins in the wooden ware business. The Bellingdon Road site extended through to Higham Road, facing Higham Mead pond. The land was drained in the early years of the 20th century, so the factory was able to extend onto this reclaimed land with a timber yard including a heavy crane, a steam engine-house and a further works for shaping the wooden brush backs.

Beechwoods originally made domestic brushes including scrubbing brushes and ones for cleaning banisters, stoves, sinks and churns. Later they also produced tooth, nail and hair brushes.

The interior of the Beechwoods factory in the late 1920s (RE)

Around 1918 they introduced a separate paintbrush division. At that time all processes were by hand.

The bristles were made of hogs' hair (pig or boar), imported mainly from China. They were classified according to the region they came from and known by such names as Grey Hankow, Chungking or Shanghai.

All the paintbrushes produced were originally round and included 'sash tool' brushes, up to 1½ inches. Bristle was bound closely with string and set into wooden handles with linseed oil and shellac. Any loose hairs were removed by tapping the brush on the edge of a bench. In the early years the whole process would have been carried out by one man. Flat varnish brushes were introduced around the 1920s, an idea imported from America. In the 1940s, distemper brushes, washing-down brushes, hogs' hair fitches, lining brushes, varnish and wall brushes were amongst the products made.

In the 1960s the majority of paintbrushes produced were still the high quality wooden-handled, pure bristle ones favoured by professional decorators. The timber used was mainly beech or birch. Locally grown beech was by this time in short supply in sufficient quantities and had to be imported from Romania, Yugoslavia or Germany.

Beechwoods ladies finishing paint brushes (RE)

Like many other factories using or storing highly inflammable materials, Beechwood's was susceptible to fire. On a Saturday morning in April 1930 a serious fire broke out in an upper storey of the building, where the brush boards were dried. Fire brigades were called out from Chesham, Amersham and Berkhamsted, a total of around 36 men. Very strong winds hampered control of the fire. Over a mile of hose was used, which had to 'travel through all sorts of back yards, passages and alleyways' before it could get anywhere near the heart of the fire. It took around two hours to bring it under control but the local brigade worked throughout the weekend to ensure it was completely extinguished. Damage was estimated at £25,000 and about two-thirds of the stock was lost.

Beechwoods after the fire of 1930 (RE)

This was in fact less devastating than earlier fires, as by this period several fire-prevention practices were in place. The factory had its own fire brigade of seven men, who all lived in the immediate area and were informed promptly. The building was evacuated and the police were also involved until the 'Shrieking Lizzie' siren called out the town brigade. The main doors from the factory to the offices were fire-proof and the most inflammable materials were stored at the far end of the wood yard as a precaution. The main machine filling shops had iron girders for fire prevention and this and the main stock warehouse were undamaged. Office staff removed safes and records to a neighbour's shed opposite the factory.

In the 1940s domestic brushware was gradually run down and had finished by the early 1960s. In 1948 Beechwoods had amalgamated with J Freeman & Co Ltd, founded in 1912, which had come out from Walthamstow in the early 1940s. Originally a toilet brush manufacturer, they had expanded to produce a wide range of mainly moulded plastic brushes. The new firm was known as **Spa Brushes Ltd.** and opened a new factory, the Freeman Works, in Alma Road. One of the products they concentrated on was plastic toothbrushes. Most of the 340 people employed then were women. Approximately 25 percent of the products were exported to over 80 countries.

An outing of Spa brushworks employees (RE)

In early 1976 the firm celebrated its centenary and anyone who had worked for the company for more than ten years received a bonus in gratitude. Later in the year a special paintbrush known as a Century Superbrush was introduced. At that time Beechwoods were producing five to six million brushes of every kind each year, including a complete range of brushes for both professional and home decorators. They were so successful in this period that they had to take on new staff to meet the increased demand. 125 men and women were employed, 100 of them in direct manufacturing. The annual turnover was around £1million. A private company for 80 years, it was by this time part of the London Rubber Company.

In 1978 the Stebrol Roller Company was acquired and all types of paint applicator could then be offered to customers. In the 1950s Stebrol had spent a lot of time and effort in encouraging professional decorators to use the paint roller, originally covered in mohair. Spa became Halex Brushware in 1971 before closing in 1981 with the loss of 28 jobs. By the late 1980s Beechwoods was within the Industrial Holdings Division of London Rubber Company International. According to a 1987 trade directory they were concentrating on making and marketing a range of paint brushes, rollers and other paint applicators. 150 people were still employed. During that year they were sold to Kalon Paints, a company based in Leeds and business moved to a new site in Halifax. They were later sold to a small consortium. However, this was unsuccessful and they went into liquidation the following year. The Chesham buildings were sold and are now occupied by B-Loony Ltd, balloon manufacturers.

Ernest Wilcock was a well-known figure in the town who worked at Beechwood's all his life. Born in 1901, he served an apprenticeship and gradually worked his way up to managing the Bellingdon Road factory. He died in 1997, aged 95. Maurice Stratford was another Beechwood's employee. He started work in 1918 as an apprentice and spent the rest of his 56-year working life there, firstly as a paintbrush maker and later as foreman of that division of the company.

Lewis Brushes Ltd was incorporated only in 1960, but it had taken over the earlier business of Arthur Oxbrough Lewis. He started in the 1920s in Vale Road, and by 1940 he was advertising as a wholesale brush manufacturer producing 'vulcanised rubber set, distemper, paint and varnish brushes'. By 1952 Lewis Brush Works was operating from Chilton Road. Lewis Brushes manufactured flat varnish and wall brushes and the major part of its output went to other brush manufacturers. Both standard lines and customer special ranges were made. During the 1940s the business employed three men, six women and two part-time older women. Hours were from 7.30am-6pm with an hour for lunch and no Saturdays. Wages for a 14-year old girl were 12s (60p) per week. Brushes were filled by hand with real bristle.

Sometime before 1915, London solicitor **W Griffin & Co** set up a brush manufacturers' business at 7a High Street for his son Sidney Herbert (**S H Griffin**). When the First World War broke out, Sidney joined the Canadian Army. He married a Canadian girl, survived the war and afterwards they settled in Chesham. By 1928 the brush business had moved to Townfield Yard, to

Chapel Brushworks at Townfield (RE)

the old Baptist chapel. This had been built in 1820 and used by the Strict and Particular Baptists until 1915, with many renowned preachers. The brush business was known locally as **Chapel Brushworks.**

In 1933 there was a devastating fire which totally destroyed the building. It broke out in the early hours of a November morning. Sidney, who lived nearby, raised the alarm but the fire quickly took hold. Flames could be seen by bus conductors and drivers as far away as Prestwood and Totteridge. By the time the fire brigade arrived they could see that the factory was doomed, so set about saving the surrounding cottages, the Zion and Hinton chapels and the warehouse of Market Square corn merchant Mr Cooper, which was filled with highly inflammable materials. The brush works' machinery, stock and records were all lost in the blaze. Sidney Griffin was not insured and some time later he took his own life.

By 1935, Sidney's son, Kenneth Griffin, had started another brush manufacturing business, **Modern Brushware Ltd**, with a partner, Mr McKenzie, in Sunnyside Road (now Buck House and occupied by B-Loony). This was still operating in 1952.

For some years after the Second World War, **Beechy Bucks Products Ltd** were also making brushes at small factories in Berkhampstead Road and Severalls Avenue and Frederick East's old factory in Townsend Road. Their 'Chromic' carpet banister brush and 'Venetian' carpet broom were exhibited at the Festival of Britain South Bank Exhibition in 1951. They also made domestic wooden ware and wood tools.

A view inside the factories (RE)

resulted in him practically losing his voice. He was a member of the Burial Board before the Cemetery was managed by the Council and he was one of the oldest members of the Conservative Association committee.

On the 1901 census, Robert was living at 112 High Street, a brush manufacturer employer, although in 1907 the business was still listed at 7a High Street as George & Sons, brush manufacturers. (These premises were occupied by brush maker W Griffin & Co in 1915).

Robert Russell
(1865-1940) (RAR)

In 1915 Harry was a wholesale brush manufacturer in Gordon Road, Waterside. He served on the Chesham Urban Council and like his father, was interested in Oddfellowship, becoming a member as a very young man. He had married Rosa Hearn in 1891. By 1935 Robert had started a business in Townsend Road. Originally very small premises at the back of the cottages fronting the road, he gradually expanded. In the early days brushes were entirely made by hand and there was outwork done at home by some of the employees. Robert's son Stanley George Robert continued the business after his father's death in 1940 and was succeeded in turn by his own son Robert Stanley George (Bob) when Stanley died in 1956. Bob, who had started in the business on leaving school at 14, served in the Royal Navy during the Second World War as a signal man, protecting convoys. Back running the family business he became ill with rheumatic fever in the 1950s. Six months recuperation gave him plenty of time to think about the future of the business. He had the foresight to diversify and began to concentrate on specialist brushes.

Robert's sons Robert Charles and Alan Stanley George joined the business as they left school. At this time most of the orders were from local councils, schools and hospitals. These included brooms for the Greater London Council (GLC), which had leather ends for extra durability, provided by local boot makers Giffard Newton. Some brushes were made for Beechwood's and others for Webb Jarratt towards the end of their time in Chesham. In the

Six generations of **Russells** have been involved in the brush industry. Charles was the first; in the 1840s he was selling brushes as well as beer from The Plough public house, White Hill. On the 1881 census his widow Ann (nee Darvell) was still there. Their son George and the two older grandsons Harry, 17 and Robert, 15, were all listed as brush makers. In 1891 George was a beer retailer & brush maker in the High Street. In 1897 George died suddenly, aged 58, from Bright's disease while living at 7a High Street. George was involved in Oddfellowship and had been one of the founders of the Chesham Lodge in 1876. He was a member of the School Board for several years. He was elected a member of the Urban District Council in 1896 and was a 'fearless speaker' but a few months before his death he had started having serious throat problems which

Russells' old factory in Townsend Road (RAR)

Bob Russell and his sons Robert and Alan (AC)

1970s, paperhangers and jamb dusters were made but these days they are produced more cheaply in China.

Bob died in 2003 at the age of 79, after fighting cancer for three years. He had been Chairman and President of Chesham Conservative Club and a member of the Royal British Legion. As an enthusiastic bowler he belonged to both Chess Vale and Chesham Park clubs.

The brothers extended the premises, and gradually took on more and more specialist work. This has included brushes for jet car washes, with the backs made of rubber but the bristles set in by hand; for painting metal constructions such as the Eiffel Tower, telegraph poles, girders, pylons and street lights. One special order was for the windmill in Paul McCartney's Sussex garden. Items are supplied to the catering industry but owing to Health & Safety Regulations now have to be constructed entirely of plastic. This includes pastry brushes, some of which are made for Lakeland Plastics. Roller-dockers for pastry-making used to be made at Reynolds woodware factory, a wooden core studded with nails. Now the Russell brothers make these with a plastic core, studded with stainless steel.

Robert (top) and Alan Russell at work in the factory, 2008

In 2006 they were approached by the BBC producers of *Extras*, who had seen the above photo. They decided they wanted to re-create this setting for the programme. This was achieved and the brothers were photographed again afterwards.

Many household brushes are supplied to the trade. A recent commission has been from a horse dentist, to produce special toothbrushes for horses. The brothers met the challenge, designing a brush made up of plastic component parts from other manufacturers. These are now sold at equine outlets and have been seen at Badminton! They have also been asked to make specialist quality flat paintbrushes for professional decorators willing to pay a premium price. When paint effects were popular they supplied specialist decorating brushes such as floggers, draggers and softeners, the latter incorporating some badger hair, also from China. Cranked-angle sash brushes are made for painting or cleaning Georgian windows. These incorporate bent and angled nails produced by local

Examples of modern products

company Servex. Nylon brushes impregnated with carbon grit are supplied to the RAF via a wholesaler. These ensure that no metal can break off whilst cleaning the control panels. The firm belongs to the British Hardware Association, which incorporated the previous brush makers' association.

Pig bristle still comes from China. There are several different types, according to the breed of pig and the local climate. Bristle from the Chungking area is considered the best quality. It is boiled, disinfected and straightened by hand then comes to a bristle merchant in London. There may well be a problem obtaining quality bristle in the future as more pork is being consumed in China. This results in the pig being killed earlier, before the bristle has grown to the best length for brush-making. Bristle is available in three natural colours – black, grey and 'white', actually a pale blonde colour. Paintbrushes are made from a mixture of bristle, some stiff, others soft, in order to produce a brush which tapers to a good point.

Brush stocks used to come from local wood ware firms James East or Frederick Leach. Now many arrive from Italy. Metal ferrules come from a company in Dudley, in the West Midlands, the last British company manufacturing them. Round ferrules and nylon bristle comes from Germany and Italy. Bristle is inserted by hand into metal templates made by a local engineer, then flooded with epoxy resin (pitch was used previously). They are then left to set under heat lamps for about an hour before being put through a 'flirting' machine, to remove any loose hairs. They are then combed by hand with a special brush maker's metal comb to ensure there are no loose hairs remaining. Finally they are stamped 'Pure Bristle' before being packed into boxes.

For several generations the Russell vision had been to specialise in quality items on a small scale rather than the large-scale manufacture of the other brush companies. Robert and Alan and their small band of eight, mostly female, part-time employees, continue this tradition to this day, meeting the challenge of survival in the 21st century. They are now the last-surviving traditional manufacturing industry in the town, but their children have gained experience of working in the business and so yet another generation will hopefully one day carry on.

Chapter 3
Building

As the town of Chesham began to develop in the late 19th and early 20th century, the demand for builders and building workers increased, with the need to house the artisan workers from the new factories.

Jesse Mead (JPM)

One who responded to this demand was Jesse Mead. Born in 1867, Jesse went into the building trade, with his brother Abel specialising in carpentry. Initially they worked with **Ben Stone**, who was well-known locally for his fine woodwork and for a timber yard in Upper High Street.

Later Jesse branched out for himself, encouraged and aided by his wife who had hitherto been a local school headmistress. By dint of hard work, considerable skill and honest endeavour they built a successful business which was in demand way outside the boundaries of Chesham. In 1909 Taylor's Farm in Newtown was put up for sale and disposed of, mainly to the Town Council for use as community allotments. However, Jesse acquired the farmhouse and yard and some adjoining land in Berkhampstead Road on which he built houses. He lived at number 176 and set up his builders yard next door. At the same time he also acquired land at the lower ends of Cameron Road and Eskdale Avenue, upon which he built a good number of houses, most of which were let to members of his workforce.

Jesse Mead's yard and houses in Berkhampstead Road (RE)

In 1914 **Jesse Mead Ltd** was formed with fellow director Edwin East. Jesse was a genial man, much loved and admired. Sadly after a long period of failing health he died in 1920 and the business was left in the hands of Mr East, who was increasingly supported by Jesse's son Cyril, who had served in the trenches in the latter part of the Second World War. Later, when the business had expanded considerably, Nos 176 and 178 were combined to form Head Office and the Contracts Offices, whilst the original office became the Small Works Dept.

A major project carried out in 1920/21 would have made Jesse very proud. 14 houses were built in 37 weeks at the foot of Bois Hill. That represents an average of 18.5 days per house to completion. With considerable advice and input from Edwin East the houses were designed by Kemp & How. They still stand today.

In the early 1960s Cyril gradually handed the business over to his two sons John and Philip who had both served their time in the construction industry with other companies. Eventually John became Managing Director and Philip was made Manager of Small Works. Throughout its lifetime the company developed and maintained a high reputation for the quality of its work. Much work was carried out in and around the town, for example the Co-op premises in The Broadway in 1899, the Co-op grand central premises in Upper High Street in 1935 and the new Red Lion pub in 1937.

Further afield a huge number of quality projects were completed over the years. In the 1920s the spire of Salisbury Cathedral was repaired and renovated. This job took immense skill and was carefully planned and supervised by Cyril Mead and the retained architect. In 1931 King George V offered the Royal Lodge at Windsor to the Duke and Duchess of York. At this time it was in a very dilapidated state and they set about transforming it into a family home. The old conservatory was demolished and a new residential wing added. All the work was carried out by Jesse Mead Ltd. Subsequently Cyril Mead was presented with a clock by the old Queen Mary. Also, in the 1930s, major works were carried out at Eton College, The Crooked Billet at Iver and at Berkhamsted School.

From 1940 to 1980 major projects involved work in Hemel Hempstead New Town, West Wycombe Park, Hughenden Manor, Wycombe Abbey (The Theatre in The Lake), St Joan of Arc School at Rickmansworth, St Clement Danes School at Chorleywood, Amersham Swimming Pool, Amersham Parish Church (re-hang bells and refit roof over the knave), Whipsnade Zoo, Waitrose No 1 in Chesham, Chenies Manor House, Latimer House and Ashridge House and College. Also term contracts were held at both RAF Halton and Chequers Court. At its peak the company employed 100 men with a further 100 sub-contractors were also employed.

In 1988, with both John and Philip wanting to retire and there being no male family members to carry on, the business was sold to Gostling's Builders Ltd but it continued on under the same name. Unfortunately by the late 1990s the business was beginning to falter and it was eventually sold on to a company in Caversham who have retained the Jesse Mead name but the Chesham works was closed down and the yard has now been redeveloped into factory units.

1920s house at the foot of Bois Hill

Started by Mr Frederick G Rust, who was later joined by Frederick G Ratcliffe, Rust & Ratcliffe gained great prestige in the early 20th century by building the select Bois Farm Estate.

Brown and Co were a sizeable joinery company and built doors, windows, frames and fencing of all kinds. In the '30s they also built Brandon's new store in the Broadway and Newtown Infants School in Berkhampstead Road.

Chesham Builders & Decorators Ltd was a workers co-operative started in 1919 and did much work around the town, particularly for the local Co-operative Retail Society. Sadly it closed in 1973.

E Greenham Ltd, a local family business incorporated in 1949, built many of the factories in Asheridge Road and Springfield Road, the Victoria Flats, the Standring Almshouses and many private dwellings in the area.

In the first half of the century it was not uncommon for building companies to also own brickyards and to make their own bricks. Brick and tile making around Chesham dates back hundreds of years and by the 1930s there were 23 brick works within five miles of Chesham Broadway. At one time Jesse Mead Ltd owned yards at Bellingdon and at Hyde Heath, whilst Rust & Ratcliffe at one time owned the Cowcroft Works in Ley Hill and another works in Copperkins Lane.

At the start of the Second World War all the brickyards were forced to close and many never reopened. However by the end of the century there were still three companies in the Chesham area making high quality facing bricks. H G Matthews in Bellingdon, purchased from Jesse Mead in 1924, Dunton Group PLC in Ley Hill close to the old Cowcroft works, and Bovingdon Brickworks in Chesham Road, Bovingdon.

Above: workers from Rust & Ratcliffe; and Keen & Greenham's works in Wey Lane, at the junction of Church Street, a site currently occupied by Gil-lec Electrical (RE)

Other major building firms in the town were **Rust & Ratcliffe** based in Higham Road, **Chesham Builders and Decorators Ltd** and **Brown & Co,** both based in Bellingdon Road and **E Greenham Ltd** (previously Keen & Greenham) of Mineral Lane.

Below: Cowcroft brickworks, Ley Hill, 1914 (JW)
and hand making bricks at Dunton brickworks, Ley Hill, 2004

Chapter 4
Engineering

By the mid-19th century, forges and blacksmiths were well established in Chesham. This was a basic and early form of engineering. Originally they were for shoeing the hundreds of horses used for drawing vehicles and working on all the local farms. Until well into the 20th century many roads and lanes were rough and stony, resulting in a short life for horseshoes. Later as motor vehicles replaced horses, the forges turned to other work. Many items were supplied for use in the building trade, for example chimney bars, hinges, fire baskets, iron gates and weather vanes. Many other common items were brought to the forge for repair. These included farm and garden implements, prams, pokers and children's hoops.

Above, top: Wallis' forge and yard in the corner of the Broadway, 1915 (AP); and Gooding's forge, Germain Street at the corner of Watermeadow, 1920s (RE)

The best known forges were **Wallis's**, in the Broadway, **Hobbs'** in Blucher Street, **Ringsell's** in Waterside by the railway bridge and **Gooding's** in Germain Street. The first three closed in the 1930s but Gooding's continued into the 1950s despite being badly damaged by a bomb in the Second World War.

Tapping's in Waterside (just before the Rose & Crown PH) made and repaired all types of harness for local horses, as did **Cox's** in the Upper High Street, another small family business. Other companies were also engaged in metalworking particularly as agricultural engineers and general mill furnishers. **Thomas Moreton and Sons**, based in Springfield Road and later Gordon Road became a 'Food Production Department' during the First World War specialising in the repair and maintenance of farm machinery. Another engineering business was started by **Sydney Cheeld** who, assisted by his son Frank, introduced the first car on to the roads of Chesham in 1904. They had made the vehicle from instructions given in a journal, *The English Mechanic and World of Science*. The company was principally involved in general engineering work for local business, repairing machinery and, in the First World War, in making shells. They also developed

Two small businesses worthy of note: Cox's, at Lacey's Yard, High Street (still trading) and Tapping's of Waterside; both were harness makers.

Derek, Alan and Peter Larkin with parents Fred and May, at the Chesham Trades Fair, 1955 (PL)

expertise in drilling and equipping artesian wells. At the end of the war, when Sydney retired, Frank joined forces with a Mr Dormer and the business continued under the name **C J Dormer and Co.** After the Second World War Frank's son Douglas joined the company and continued the family tradition in engineering with the name reverting to **F Cheeld Ltd**.

In 1925 Thomas Hindmarsh formed Modern Wheel Drive Ltd, with offices in Westminster and works in Slough, for the design and manufacture of ship's gearboxes. The offices were bombed in 1941 and the firm, hastily looking for a roof over its head, moved into 'Wendy', a bungalow in Springfield Road, and became yet another part of Chesham's war work. At that time, the company was solely engaged on designing and making gearboxes for the navy. The tank landing craft used for invasion purposes, hundreds of air-sea rescue ships, minesweepers and others were equipped with gearboxes that had been designed, manufactured and tested in Bucks. Government demands and rapid expansion of output necessitated larger premises and in November 1942 Lindo Lodge in Stanley Avenue was purchased to house the design engineers and draughtsmen. Two other houses in Stanley Avenue were used to house the accounts and general office staff. After the war, major export business was developed with Thomas Hindmarsh's unique 'oil operated' designs being in demand all over the world.

Lindo Lodge had three floors, with the ground floor then set aside for Mr Hindmarsh, his secretary and the live-in housekeeper. The first floor provided offices for the sales department and the technical director whilst the draughtsmen were in the eaves on the second floor. By the 1960s two huts in the garden housed the technical department, surrounded by lawns and trees. For the bearings in the gearboxes, white metal was used, an expensive commodity even in those days and it was stored in a secure building at The Lodge. Every Friday a van left Chesham for the Slough factory, supposedly in secret, with the next weeks

consignment of white metal. At one time 75 people worked in the Stanley Avenue facilities, but in 1967 the company left Chesham when all staff moved into a purpose-built factory on the Bath Road in Slough. In the second half of the century a number of other general engineering companies were established in Chesham and provided valuable employment for the local people.

During the Second World War, Fred Larkin was employed in aircraft production. At the end of hostilities he and his wife May established an engineering business, **Larkin Forge Ltd**, in Burnt Oak, Edgware. They came to live in Chesham in 1947 and transferred their business here three years later. The company took over a disused cart shed and stables in Springfield Road. The cart shed was in a very dilapidated state, so a new building was erected over and around the old structure, which was then dismantled. Business continued throughout the whole operation. Meanwhile the old stables were stripped, panelled and converted into offices and stores. The company became a significant employer in the town with 50 staff manufacturing laminated road springs for cars, buses, coaches and commercial vehicles, as well as providing a spring reconditioning service to fleet operators. It also made agricultural tines for machine manufacturers and spring steel table tops for mining tables, developed by Dowty Mining.

In 1973 the company joined forces with Jonas Woodhead of Leeds, the largest vehicle suspension maker in Europe. The Larkin family left the business in 1976 and built two warehouses south of the Larkin Forge factory and established Chesham Storage and Distribution and shortly afterwards, Larkin Distributive Services Ltd. The business finally closed in 2000 and a seat, presented by the Larkin family, was erected on The Moor, opposite Christchurch, remembering all the staff who had worked for the company over the latter half of the century.

In 1947 Mr Horace Bailey, who had previously worked as a toolmaker for Hoover, started his own company in Willesden. He

Lindo Lodge in Stanley Avenue, 1947 (RB)

Horace Bailey's Chiltern Instruments, Higham Mead factory (RS)

bought three shops and converted them to workshops under the name Porters Printing Accessories. He gathered a team of 40 employees together and they made duplicators and office equipment. The business was not successful, so six years later he moved to Chesham and started a new venture. Premises were rented in Waterside opposite the Post Office and a precision engineering company, called **Porters Holdings Ltd**, was started, manufacturing components for the aircraft industry. The firm commenced jig boring, tool making and prototype work and an expensive precision machine was purchased with the proceeds of the sale of the Willesden equipment.

The first customer was Rolls Royce Aero Engines Division. The business went from strength to strength and in 1956 a piece of land was purchased in Higham Mead and building commenced for a new factory. This was completed in 1960 when Mr Bailey and his staff of 25 moved in. Specialist gauges were added to the product range and many orders were won from the major aircraft and aerospace companies. Within a year the workforce had expanded to 60.

By the 1970s the company had changed its name to **Chiltern Instruments Ltd,** by which time it was a leading precision engineering organisation, specialising in the manufacture of high precision, complex components to very high quality standards. Services offered were material procurement, milling, turning, grinding, component assembly/fitting, heat and process treatments. Amongst products made were high precision printing blocks for bank cheques. The company continued to expand; it developed a very high reputation and employed about 70 people at its peak. Ultimately the business was taken over by APL of Guildford but closed in February 1994.

Above: Chiltern Instruments' machine room; and right: some of its precision products (RS)

In the 1970s **Reliant Tooling Ltd** of Asheridge Road were providing work for more than 60 people, engaged in making machines for the textile industry. Success in this field brought them a Queens Award for Industry in 1974. Tougher times a decade later resulted in them switching to making window blinds for their sister company Reliant Venetian Blinds Ltd in Wales. By this time, Chesham Engineering and Pentagon Products were operating small engineering jobbing shops at the north end of the town.

Workers at Moyes Foundry, 1915 (RE)

Foundries also existed in the town for most of the century. In the early part they were run by **Edward Urry** in Berkhampstead Road and **James Moyes** in George Street (later **Moyes & Redding**)

After the Second World War, **Amac Refinements Ltd** were operating in Eskdale Avenue producing hardware and small castings in various metals to be followed by **A E Clements Ltd,** whose foundry produced boxes and levers for electrical equipment, traffic sign components and domestic appliances such as the mop. They also developed special dies for aluminium alloy propellers for small boats.

More recently a foundry has operated in Bellingdon Road. Originally operated by **J G Statter & Co**, the electrical switchgear company based in Little Chalfont, it was taken over by **Draycast Foundries** in 1970. Terry and Bob Nagle started the company in Wooburn Green in 1964 and on moving to Chesham soon installed new electrical and induction furnaces. Since then the company has developed into one of the foremost jobbing foundries in Europe, specialising in high quality castings for a broad range of engineering and commercial applications. These include precision sand castings and pressure tight castings for the fluid handling industry.

In 1931 a company for the employment of disabled people was started in Oldham Street, Manchester by Mr A Hill, himself a disabled man. It went under the name 'The Limbless and Disabled Servicemen's Demonstrations' and initially produced rolled gold jewellery. The vigour with which these men worked was quite astounding. Before long they supplied some rolled gold items to the Royal Family. Then with the assistance of Sir Frederick Marquis and Sir Simon Marks the firm got its foot on the commercial ladder when it was granted sales space in both John Lewis and Marks & Spencer stores. Similar factories opened in London, Burnley and Birmingham and steady progress was made up to and during the Second World War.

In 1944 the Government introduced the Disabled Persons (Employment) Act and accepted their national responsibility for training handicapped people. With the establishment of Government-run Remploy factories there was no longer such a need for Mr Hill's factories. He decided to close the facilities in London, Manchester and Burnley and to open a small factory in Bellingdon Road, Chesham under the name **Servex Ltd**. Here engineering and electroplating work was developed while costume jewellery manufacture continued in Birmingham.

The company not only survived to the end of the century but is still in business today. It has continued to be a precision engineering 'Trade Shop' and to also offer a full range of finishes in the electroplating and metal finishing department. It is a family-run firm with a caring concern for customers, workforce and the environment.

Chapter 5
Food and drink

In early times Chesham was an agricultural town with much rearing of sheep, pigs and cattle and the growing of corn for grinding at the mills. This continued until well into the 20th century as did the growing of watercress and the brewing of beer. Later, companies producing other foodstuffs and drinks came to the area.

Watercress

In Victorian times, Chesham and the Chess Valley became well-known for watercress growing. By the River Chess, artesian wells were drilled down to a depth of about 130 feet into the aquifer to gain a steady flow of the unique hard, chalky water in which watercress thrives. By the beginning of the century, 30 acres of watercress beds were well established, mostly around Waterside, Bois Moor Road and Weir House Mill. There were other beds in Higham Mead, Pednor Road, Missenden Road, Waterside and at the junction of Red Lion Street with Amersham Road. The majority of the cultivated product was sent by train in large willow hampers to Covent Garden Market in London and to the large towns in the North of England. **William Puddephatt** was a pioneer of watercress growing in Chesham. His son in law **Sidney Gamester** carried on production at Weir House Mill whilst **Beckley and Holliman** dominated in the Bois Moor area. **Darvell's** watercress beds were in Waterside just past the railway bridge in an area now concreted over as a factory car park

The local industry suffered a sudden collapse in the 1930s following an unfounded report that an outbreak of typhoid in Croydon was attributed to watercress. Business revived in the austere

Picking watercress in the Chess Valley (RE)

years of the Second World War only to suffer another gradual decline thereafter, although watercress was still available in Chesham Market in the 1990s from **Andy Palmer's** small scale cressbed on the millpond behind the swimming pool. The one surviving watercress bed producing in this area is downstream at Sarratt.

Jack Holliman (of Beckley & Holliman) at Watford Station (RE)

Beer, cider and other drinks

In the 19th century Chesham boasted numerous public houses and beer shops whose landlords brewed their own distinctive beer. There were also several small dedicated breweries throughout the town. In the 1840s Thomas and James Nash commenced brewing as a sideline in the High Street. Their business developed into a full-scale operation and in 1895 the business was incorporated as **The Chesham Brewery Ltd.** For the next 60 years it was an important part of the town's manufacturing industry, employing many local men. A merger with Hopcraft and Norris of Brackley in 1946 resulted in a name change to **Chesham & Brackley Breweries Ltd.**

A deep well under the brewery supplied the spring water which gave a distinctive taste to the beer. Many local favourites such as Chesham Bitter and Raven Stout were produced. Sadly the brewery struggled to compete with the move to bottled beers, was closed in 1957 and demolished in 1961.

In addition to traditional beers and ales, in the early part of the 20th century local people could also obtain home brewed ginger beer, mineral water and 'pop' from **Ellen Wallington & Son** in Waterside and cider, fruit wines and cordials from **The Mid Bucks Cider Factory**, run by J D Pallett and Co, in nearby Buckland Common.

Chesham & Brackley Brewery ales (CS)

Wallington's delivering soft drinks to The Lamb in the Broadway (RE)

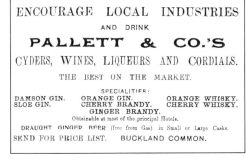

Below: View over Chesham Brewery in 1961, shortly before its demolition (RE)

Cocoa and chocolate

In 1828 a Dutchman named Coenrand Johannes Van Houten invented a formula for powdered cocoa that was easily soluble in hot water or milk. He designed a method for the removal of superfluous fat by pressurisation, enabling conversion to a powder. This was such a considerable improvement on the previously insoluble and indigestible cocoa lump product, that King William I of the Netherlands granted a 'Letters Patent' to the Van Houten organisation for the production of powdered chocolate. Business expansion followed quickly, such that a larger factory was required and in 1850 the Dutch Van Houten works was established at Weesp. As the 20th century began, the introduction of mechanisation enabled the production of cocoa and chocolate to increase rapidly. Markets opened up across the world particularly in Europe and the United States and a factory was established in London. However, with the commencement of the Second World War **Van Houten Ltd** was forced to evacuate and in 1939 it came to Chesham. The first premises consisted of some outbuildings at Bury Farm, rented from Andy Melville, and gradually other premises around

VAN HOUTEN LTD.
COCOA & CHOCOLATE
MANUFACTURERS
LONDON & CHESHAM

Van Houten's Bellingdon Road premises

the town were taken over. By 1950 Van Houten Ltd was dispersed throughout the area on eleven different sites.

This created its own problems which were not resolved until 1953 when the site in Asheridge Road, formerly occupied by George Williams clothing company, was purchased. The business continued to grow and employed 300 people in the town at one time. However, in 1962, the company was taken over by W R Grace Co of America and the inevitable rationalisation soon followed. In 1964 the production of cocoa powder, confectionery and assorted chocolates was closed down, with the loss of 60 jobs. Chocolate manufacture continued until 1966 when the company left the town. The Van Houten brand name, still in use today, has been transferred several times, most recently in 1990 from the German chocolate manufacturer Jacobs Suchard to Phillip Morris.

Mushrooms

Mushrooms were grown commercially in the area for much of the century. From 1958 to 1988 **Buckingham Mushrooms** were growers in Lycrome Road. At the peak, 100 employees were involved in producing 40,000lbs per week.

Poultry

For most of the 20th century Chesham was well served with supplies of poultry, originally ducks, then chickens and, latterly, turkeys. Many ducks were bred alongside the River Chess on Chesham Moor. Ralph Hills and Fred Harding were two of the well known duck breeders in

Waller's Aylesbury ducks

this area. Two duck farms were also established in Chartridge Lane, one of them **Waller's,** which still survives today. In the 1920s and early 1930s Waller's business thrived and turkeys and laying chickens were added to their range.

In 1934 Mervyn How started keeping chickens and ducks as a hobby in Missenden Road. Later an enforced move saw him set up in business in Chesham Vale. He could not have foreseen that for the rest of the century he and his son Ron would become pioneers in the UK turkey industry, producing the first early-hatched turkeys, conducting the first freezing of turkeys on the farm, and doing experimental work on drugs and supplements for turkeys. **Chessovale Turkeys** soon gained a very good reputation for the quality of their meat. Ron and Mervyn became founder members of the British Turkey Federation, as did Andy Melville of Bury Farm, Pednor Road.

Andy had come to Chesham in 1937 after farming in Abingdon and initially was involved with pedigree herds of cattle and pigs on his 600 acre estate. Very soon chickens and turkeys were introduced and the business assumed the title **PP Poultry.**

Like the Hows, he was very innovative. He introduced a mail order business offering 7lb birds for 30 shillings each, sent by post ready for the oven. Later Andy took over Bury House and began selling turkey pies and turkey soup. He employed 100 workers at one time. Sadly his business ran into trouble in the early '60s, and despite financial restructuring and a name change to **Melville Turkeys**, the company folded in 1964.

White turkeys at P P Poultry, Pednor Road (PM)

Chapter 6
Plastics

Just as the electronics industry did, so the plastics industry developed rapidly in the second half of the century. New materials and manufacturing technologies enabled an enormous range of innovative products and parts to be made in plastic, which became the most widely used material in the world.

One of the first plastics companies in Chesham was **B Z Products Ltd** who made containers for the pharmaceutical industry at the Empire Works in Station Road.

Later **A F Grover & Co Ltd** moved into the old Co-operative boot factory in Higham Road, where 30 employees were involved in injection moulding of high quality components and packaging items. It closed in 1984.

Meanwhile, next door in the old electricity power station in Higham Mead, Brian Harris started a company in 1972 called **In Blow Form**. At its peak, about 35 people were employed in blow moulding products and components for industrial use. Major customers included Hoover and the Ford Motor Company. The business was taken over in 1993 and the Chesham factory closed in 2000, when all work was moved to Slough.

Another injection moulding company, **Chess Plastics Ltd,** was originally started in Tring in 1967, by local man Malcolm Olden and his wife Marilyn. In 1978 it moved from High Wycombe to a new 5000 sq ft factory in Bellingdon Road. With new machines and a workforce of 35 the business prospered and grew. Major customers at this stage included Max Factor cosmetics and Walls ice cream.

The company moved to Droitwich, Worcestershire in 1990 at the request of its then major customer Vax Appliances. Subsequently the site was taken over by another moulding company **Kaden Plastics**.

Brian Harris in his Higham Road factory (AC)

Malcolm Olden sealing the deal to buy two new 150 tonne Battenfiled machines for his new Chesham factory (courtesy Chess Plastics Ltd)

Chapter 7
Printing

The Reading family started their business in Chesham in 1835 as a stationers, newagents and library. It was J W Reading who brought the first powered printing press, driven by gas, to the town shortly before 1900. Before that, all printing was done on Caxton type hand presses, using technology that dated back to the 15th century. A system of 'movable type' and 'letterpress' continued to be used, where individual pieces of metal type, each with an individual letter of the alphabet (Monotype), were composed to create text which was inked up and put on paper. Later, whole lines of type were cast in metal (Linotype), making the process of composition more efficient.

In 1900 the business was taken over by A T Roberts & Sons Ltd, with Carlton Roberts as managing director. From this point on the print works became known as **The Carlton Press**. It was located in the Broadway, with a factory extension in Waterside. In 1901 it was engaged in Government contracts and also printed *The War Office Times* and *The Naval Review*. The Carlton Press was sold to F J Wilson & Sons Ltd in 1912 but the trading name remained.

Elsewhere in the town, several attempts were made to establish a newspaper for Chesham, including the ill-fated *Chesham Advertiser*, first produced by J E King of 7 Red Lion Street in 1892. A High Wycombe company, Messrs Butler & Son, published *The Chesham Examiner, Amersham & Rickmansworth Times* in 1889 from 9 High Street, Chesham. In 1899 the publication moved to 110 Church Street, where it was printed by Henry George Bonner. In the same year, **Page & Thomas**, a Chesham printing business dealing with local organisations and industry, took over the newspaper and moved it to 16 Germain Street, where it remains today, known since 1906 as *The Bucks Examiner*.

Page & Thomas looked to expand, but it was not until the 1920s that Mr Thomas, a Christian man, made a move into religious literature that was to change the company's fortunes. From a simple beginning with 1,000 copies of the Children's Special Service Mission's *Daily Notes*, a manuscript devised by Mr J H Hubbard of Chesham, the firm went on to print hundreds of thousands of magazines, teachers' journals and Sunday School texts to be distributed nationwide, and literally millions of the *Golden Bells* hymn books for the international market. Later these were published under the imprint 'The Chesham Press'.

In 1939 Novello's, the music publishers, became financially involved with Page & Thomas, as a means of safeguarding their London interests in case of bombing during the war. This brought additional work, machinery and business to the Chesham company which necessitated expanding into the old Hayes boot factory in Waterside. *The Bucks Examiner* expanded in unison, and under the editorship of Frank Hiddleston, affectionately known as 'Spec', its circulation increased from 900 when he took up the post in 1904, to 9,500 when he retired in 1954. Large factory extensions were added at Germain Street in 1957 and 1961, with the latest wire stitching and guillotining machines, and a consolidation of the business. In 1960 *The Bucks Examiner* became the first weekly in the country to carry a full-colour page advertisement, and full-colour news photograph.

In contrast to Page & Thomas, the years of the Second World War had been difficult for the Carlton Press, due to paper shortages and scarcity of labour. After the war, however, the business flourished and considerable printing was done for the National Magazine Company and other major publishers. In May 1947, Richard Askew was employed at the Carlton Press at £250 per annum. He was assistant to his father who was made

'The Carlton ladies on the spree', 1918 (RE)

Top: The composing room at Page & Thomas, showing the type cases, and above: printing on an 8-Crown Perfector at the Waterside branch. Right: a typical religious text in which Page & Thomas specialised at their 'Chesham Press' (LR)

Page & Thomas works, Germain Street, illustrated in 1929. Note the river running along the front, as well as by Duck Alley to the left

Managing Director following the death of Mr Wilson. In the 1950s the Askews part purchased the company and became directors.

In January 1952 there was a disastrous fire at The Carlton Press with many fire brigades called to the Broadway. Recovery from this took time but was accomplished after considerable effort and the business continued. In 1958 the business was sold again to Davies Investments, who also purchased Page & Thomas from Novello & Co. The Carlton Press and Page & Thomas, with the *Bucks Examiner*, came together as The Davies Press. However, this was a particularly traumatic time, with a Labour Government credit squeeze, with the final result that liquidators sold the business to Websters Publications Ltd and in 1968 The Carlton Press and Page & Thomas merged to form **The Chesham Press Ltd**. Richard (Dick) Askew, of the Carlton Press, remained as Managing Director until 1987.

Sheet-fed lithographic printing was first introduced as a replacement to letterpress at the end of the 1960s. Production was rationalised and amalgamated in the Germain Street premises. At this time, 'web-offset' printing was also beginning to come within the scope of medium-sized companies and the task of reassessing requirement for the new plant was given to Mr H L Livermore, deputy managing director. After considerable research it was decided in 1970 to install a rotary web-offset press, on which printing plates were mounted on a rotating cylinder that came into contact with a rotating roll of paper. This gave the capability of printing up to 48 pages at 18,000 copies an hour.

At its height, The Chesham Press had about 140 staff working directly or indirectly on print production, with double-day shifts in most production departments. To relieve pressure on the composing department, a complete range of photo-typesetting equipment was installed in 1975. In 1988, the editorial staff of *The Bucks Examiner* embraced the desktop publishing revolution and replaced their typewriters with office computers.

The Chesham Press ended its life in Chesham in 1989 with the closure of Chess Valley Origination in Sunnyside Road. This was the typesetting and page planning department of I T Matters, which had bought The Chesham Press in 1985. The Germain Street plant was demolished in 1990, with printing transferred to Raans Road, Amersham. Various buy-outs of the newspaper title have ensued.

There were many other smaller printing operations in the town during the century, for example **Nashleigh Printers Ltd**, which was operating in the 1930s and '40s, and **Norman & Son** of Hivings Hill, the town's leading signwriters for many decades. **Blundells Printers** of East Street was part of the bookshop and stationers in Market Square. In 1971 Mr Blundell sold it to Bill Phillips, who had worked at both Page & Thomas and the Carlton Press. With his business partner Alan Bickerton, Bill installed a 4-colour litho press, and an IBM composer – the forerunner of desktop publishing. The business was sold in 1981 and became **Prestige Press**, which is still trading. Alan went on to become a director of **Neolith Offset Ltd**, which operated at Higham Mead from 1968 to 2002. Another small print works is **Orbitpress**, establised in 1982, with early links to the Print Shop in Station Road. Originally based in the High Street, then Red Lion Street, it is now settled in Market Square.

Several larger local print firms were established from the late 1960s to service The Chesham Press, and as a direct result of the expansion of the print industry in nearby Watford. **Derek Croxson Ltd** and **J & M Nixon Printers Ltd** took over the two Waterside factories vacated by The Chesham Press in the 1970s and early '80s. Croxsons was originally a plate-making operation, but the Wright family expanded into prepress and printing from a base in Moor Road, until closure in 2008. The Nixon family business evolved into The Print Centre, now based at Berkhamsted, while two of its employees set up **Ink Link** in 1988, still trading in Chesham. By the 1990s, printing was one of the major industries in Chesham, but declined rapidly in the new century due to competition from outside the area and consolidation of larger print firms. Chesham retains several print firms, many now operating computer to plate technology, alongside digital presses.

Right: rotary web-offset printing at the Chesham Press Ltd in the 1970s

Chapter 8
Retail

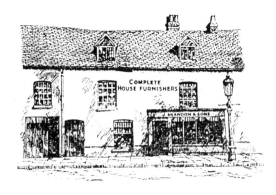

Chesham had long been a town with many small shops centred on the High Street, Church Street and the Broadway and, as it entered the 20th century, two organisations which had started in the 19th century came to dominate the vistas of the Broadway and Upper High Street.

Co-op milk van, 1930s (RE)

The **Chesham Equitable Co-operative Society** had been established in 1875 and at the turn of the century had just commenced operations in its new central premises in the Broadway. Built by Jesse Mead, these premises covered an area of 1,036 square yards with a frontage of 43 feet. Initially there were grocery and butcher's stores with adjoining drapery and shoe shops. To the rear was a large bakehouse, a slaughterhouse, a storeroom and stables for three horses. There was also room for pens for beasts, pigs and sheep. On the second floor was a function room, Equity Hall, a committee room and the secretary's office.

As time went on the Society began to dominate retailing in Chesham. New shops were opened in Newtown in 1912 and in Upper High Street in 1921. Soon it was delivering groceries, bread, milk and coal throughout the town and surrounding areas as well as adding clothes, furniture, household goods and confectionery to its range of products. Banking, insurance and funeral services were also offered. The idea of customer share ownership and the pay out of dividends was really proving popular. A greengrocery shop was opened at 54 Broadway in 1933.

With such rapid growth it was no surprise that even more facilities were required and grand new central premises were built in Upper High Street, opening in 1935. Again these were built by Jesse Mead Ltd with electrical work this time by another local firm, D L Chittenden.

Having taken over the Wycombe Co-operative Society in 1920 and the Tring Society in 1948, for a large part of the 20th century 'The Co-op' was not only a major supplier of goods and services, it was also a major employer in the town and, as it expanded, provided much work locally for the building industry. Sadly the Co-operative movement generally did not continue to compete successfully with the coming of the supermarkets in the '60s and '70s and by 1984 all Co-op shops and services in Chesham had closed.

Co-op lorry decorated for the Co-op fête and fancy dress parade, 1927 (ML)

Co-op shop in the Broadway, 1920, and illustration by Madeleine Fletcher of the grand central premises of 1935

Other long-established retailers

Darvells' bakery, established 1838 by William and Sarah Darvell at 14 Church Street, and still trading in the High Street.

Wright's corn & seed merchants of Germain Street, established 1888; closed in recent years *(pictured)*.

Cox the Saddlers – Herbert Cox first came to Chesham in the 1890s to work for William Lacey. Still trading at Lacey's Yard, High St.

Mayo & Hawkes, cycle dealers, established at 16 Red Lion Street in 1928; closed 2006.

Turner & Browning, opticians, established 1933.

Pearces hardware, est. 1938

In 1924, H R (Ray) Harborne joined the business and, when in 1936 the Brandon brothers retired, he bought it, retaining both the name and the old tradition. Many a local young man learned the furniture and carpet trade whilst in the employ of Brandon's.

When Mr Harborne Senior died in 1971, his son Leslie, who had joined the company in 1947, took over and ran the business until 1977. He eventually sold out and the business closed in 1980.

Opposite page, top: the original Brandon shop at 84 Broadway;
above: advertisement from the Brandon catalogue of 1923;
above, right: Brandon's grand premises, built 1923

Also dominating the scene in the Broadway for much of the century was the firm of **J Brandon & Sons.** Originally a small business in Tring run by Mr J Brandon, his three sons came to Chesham in 1896 and opened a shop at 84 Broadway. They offered a complete household furnishing and removals business as well as carpet beating and mattress re-making. The brothers upgraded the shop and continued to work from this site until 1923 when the three adjacent cottages were demolished and a grand new store was built (86-94 Broadway). Space was also taken for showrooms at one time in the Broadway at the site of the old Ivory Coffee Tavern and also in the Palace Cinema complex.

Above: inside Brandon's store, 1972, and
below: the second Brandon shop at 84 Broadway (LH)

Chapter 9
Services

As well as companies making products, Chesham has been home to many businesses that provided services. These were not only important to their customers, but also to the local economy and the employment market. Services offered ranged from laundering to warehousing and distribution, haulage, procurement and specialised advice.

Above and left: ladies of the ironing room, Royal Bucks Laundry, c1905 (RE)

Laundering

The industrial revolution completely changed the process of washing laundry. By the 20th century the development of machines, detergents and soaps had resulted in the establishment of commercial laundries. Two emerged in Chesham,

The Chesham Laundry opened in 1902 in Eskdale Avenue (later to evolve into **The Perfection Laundry,** run by George Robjent) and the larger **Royal Bucks Laundry** of Waterside opened in 1905 on the site of Shute's former silk mill. The Royal Bucks was owned and run by the Jackson family and boasted a fleet of 25 vans which were instantly recognisable by their blue livery and little Dutch girl logo. The laundry boxes were

an equally familiar sight. Weekly collections and deliveries were made over a wide area and resulted at one time in employment for 180 females and 40 males.

Despite additional dry cleaning services, both companies suffered after 1945 as affluent homes acquired washing machines and dryers. The Perfection Laundry (later known as the Green Hill Laundry) closed in the 1960s and the Royal Bucks in 1973.

Laundry packing girls, early 1930s (JA). *The familiar RBL laundry basket is pictured left*

Above: Royal Bucks Laundry, 1914 and below: in the early 1970s (RE)

Market research

By the 1960s, data processing devices were beginning to transform the information technology industry. This development enabled Bedford Attwood, a gentleman farmer from Ballinger, to set up a leading market research company, **Attwood Statistics**, that specialised in television audience measurements and consumer surveys. Bedford, a former director of Plessey, was an entrepreneur, also owned an antique shop, was an expert on clocks and watches and a man of considerable intellect. The company's main offices were in London and Berkhamsted but, in the 1970s, 50 employees were busy processing consumer data at Panel House (now Buck House) in Sunnyside Road. At the time it was the largest market research company in Europe. The business was sold in 1979 and moved to Eastcote.

Procurement and advice

Started in Knightsbridge in 1962, **Agricultural Central Trading** (ACT) came to Chesham a year later. A farmers' co-operative, launched by the National Farmers' Union, the business occupied two floors of offices in White Hill where 180 people were employed at its peak. The main business provided farmers with an efficient procurement service for items such as fertilisers and farm equipment, but also offered advice and training. The company later relocated to a smaller office in the Broadway.

The ACT offices in White Hill (RE)

Warehousing, distribution and haulage

In the latter half of the 20th century Doug McMinn was one of the best known and best loved businessmen in Chesham. He first came to the town in 1916 when his father, who was in the army, moved his wife and three children out of London. Doug left school at 14 and immediately got involved in trading. He bought reject brooms, brushes, pots and pans and sold them at country markets. He collected firewood and sold it to local people. With the proceeds he bought an old bicycle which enabled him to extend his activities.

After the Second World War, Doug opened his first hardware shop in Bellingdon Road, later moving to 105 High Street and finally in 1950 to Weir House Mill in Latimer Road where **D McMinn Ltd** became firmly established. Although in the early days the company invented and produced a mop and a clothes prop which were very successful, it developed subsequently as a factoring company, storing and distributing domestic hardware, ironmongery and garden products to independent hardware and DIY shops and garden centres. In 1967 Mr McMinn gave 75% of the

company's shares to 40 of his long serving employees. Seven years later, when the business was sold to **Tricentrol Oil Co** those lucky people shared £1M. The other 160 employees were not forgotten – they

McMinn's base at Latimer Road (BB)

shared £250,000 calculated on earnings and length of service. Before the end of the century the business was sold again to **Decco Ltd.**

The firm of **Langley-Smith & Co (Oils and Turpentine) Ltd** was founded in London in 1907. The company moved its warehouse and filling plant to Chesham in 1961 and its offices two years later. From its Langlow Works in Asheridge Road, turpentines, white spirit, distillates, creosote, tar, vegetable oils and lubricants were distributed to the building, paint and chemical industries. Some 75 people were employed by the company, which later changed its name to **Langlow Products Ltd**.

A short distance up Asheridge Road on the other side of the street was **SPD Ltd**, who came to the town in 1957, initially to look after the distribution requirements of companies like Unilever, Whitbread and Batchelors. 170 people were employed in the 1960s. In 1984 the depot became a central distribution centre for Kellogg's. From the Chesham warehouse the well known breakfast cereals – Corn Flakes, All-Bran, Rice Krispies and Coco Pops – were delivered to all the major multiple store outlets. In 1985 the company was acquired by National Freight Consortium who a few years later combined SPD Ltd with Roadline and National Carriers Ltd to form **Exel Logistics**. Following rationalisation the company left Chesham in the mid 1990s.

SPD Ltd warehouse and offices in Asheridge Road. Langlow Works is bottom centre of picture (AB)

Many general hauliers operated from the town throughout the century. Early on these were timber carriers such as **William Darvell** in Springfield Road, **Herbert Groves** and **John Woodley** in Bois Moor Road. **Thomas Hewitt Catling** started a general haulage company in the late 19th century. Originally located in Market Square, it later moved to the junction of Amersham Road and Moor Road, where it continued into the 1950s when it became part of the nationalised **British Road Services**. By the 1970s **Harry Hearn's** business had evolved into **Cave Wood (Transport) Ltd,** offering direct road services to Europe from their base in Bois Moor Road.

Douglas McMinn and some of his long-serving employees, 1974 (BB)

Thomas Catling lorry (JMB)

Chapter 10
Textiles

Ladies' hosiery and underwear

As mentioned in the section on Toys, opposite, the Happy Day Toy Company's brief life was ended when it became the **Marie Antoinette Hosiery** factory in Severalls Avenue in the early 1920s. Principally silk stockings were made. This continued until 1931 when **The Bucks Manufacturing Co Ltd,** under Managing Director Mr W Thorpe, took over the business from the Selfridge Co. A complete range of three-part ladies' under-garments were added to the product line, based largely on silk and botany wool. Over 1,000 garments per week were dispatched from this factory.

The skills required for this type of work were quite new to Chesham but the local workforce, mainly young ladies, adapted quickly and soon developed the necessary competence. The company left Chesham in 1938.

Moving stock into 99 Waterside (courtesy W Williams & Son, Bread St, London)

Textile distribution

Another company bearing the Williams name came to Chesham during the Second World War. **W Williams & Son Ltd** moved into the factory in Waterside, built for Thomas Wright's woodwork in the 19th century, after their premises in Hackney were badly damaged by fire during the blitz in 1941. They were part of the textile distribution industry that was concentrated in the City of London. They specialised in haberdashery products, neckwear and trimmings, knitwear, fur and fancy goods, for which they needed lots of warehouse space. They secured additional premises in Pinner, Northwood Hills and Little Chalfont. They also bought two houses in Chesham, including 'Germains,' which provided some staff accomodation.

Tassels and trimmings

After the war another textile company, **Kerr Brothers Ltd,** came to Chesham and was based in the old Town Hall. They manufactured braiding, trimmings and silk fringes, and provided lots of home-based work for housewives.

Also in the 1950s, **Arthur Hyatt & Son Ltd** were producing artificial silk trimmings in Alexander Street.

Stocking manufacture at Severalls Avenue (RE)

Kerr Brothers Ltd in the old Town Hall (RE)

Utility clothing

George Williams and Co Ltd came to Chesham at the start of the Second World War and initially moved into one of the outbuildings at Bury Farm. In 1942 they took over the building in Severalls Avenue, mentioned above, and continued to make utility clothing, mainly for juveniles. The business thrived under the leadership of managing director, Mr L Moritzson, to such an extent that after the war, a beautiful new factory was built in Asheridge Road, and the company relocated in 1946. It was laid out for mass production, covering the complete process from fabric to finished garments. The building became known as the 'Garden Factory' because it was surrounded by attractive flower beds, grassy plots and banks, and a productive vegetable patch which supplied much produce for the works canteen and the 95 employees. The company left the town in late 1951.

Chapter 11
Toys

In the 19th century, many children's toys were produced commercially in Chesham. The wooden ware manufacturers produced hoops, spades, cricket bats, etc as well as their range of household goods.

Teddy bear, top:
Master Teddy, 1915
(courtesy Lucky Bears Ltd)
Teddy bear, bottom:
Chiltern Toys' Hugmee bear

Dolls's house manufacture at Moor Road

At the start of the 20th century, Thomas Wright's in Newtown had a section called **The Chesham Wooden Toy Works.** However, in 1914 a new entrant, **Selfridge & Co Ltd,** commenced specialist toy manufacture in the three-storey building in Severalls Avenue (circled above), previously used by George Barnes & Sons Ltd for boot manufacturing. They made mainly wooden toys under the name **The Happy Day Toy Company.** Today the site is occupied by Nashleigh Court. Manufacture continued for eight years until Selfridge switched to making silk stockings (see previous Textile section).

Meantime, another toy manufacturer came to Chesham. Its roots went back to Germany in the 1880s when the firm of Eisenmann & Co was founded by Josef Eisenmann. It was an export agency dealing largely in fancy goods and toys. In 1908 Josef's son-in-law, Leon Rees, approached the English soft toy manufacturers J K Farnell & Co and persuaded them to begin making teddy bears. In 1913, Josef set up his own factory at 101 Bellingdon Road, in part of the building occupied for many years by Beechwood Brushes Ltd. Initially dolls were produced for the *London Evening News.* Subsequently manufacturing changed to other toys. Their first bear, 'The Master Teddy' was made in 1915. He was a funny looking creature with googly eyes, dressed cotton body and a red tongue. Only his head and paws were made from mohair.

When Josef died in 1919, Leon inherited the business and he decided to go into partnership with Harry Stone, an old friend from Farnell's. They formed **H G Stone & Co** and moved to larger premises in Waterside, and 'Chiltern Toys' was born. In 1921 the company opened a second factory at Tottenham, North London and the House of Rees was formed, comprising L Rees & Co, the parent company, H G Stone & Co and the **Amersham Woodware and Sports Works.** This latter company also used part of 101 Bellingdon Road as a warehouse and, from its factory at the junction of Moor Road and Amersham Road, produced a large range of wooden toys and sports goods.

The Waterside factory was almost entirely staffed by single young ladies. In those days it was not deemed acceptable to work once you were married. From the Amersham Works the range of wheeled toys included dolls' pushchairs, pedal cars, pole carts, wheelbarrows and stuffed animals on wheels. Wooden toys included dolls' houses and castles, dolls' house furniture, train sets, blackboards and easels and a folding playpen in polished beech with coloured beads. Among the sports goods were table tennis sets, cricket bats and tennis rackets. At one time this factory employed 120 people and 600 tennis rackets were dispatched weekly.

In 1923, Chiltern Toys introduced their most famous design of teddy bear, the 'Hugmee' and in 1925 the firm took over another range of soft toys called 'Panurge Pets'. The business went from strength to strength. In 1929 another new factory, aptly named Chiltern Works, was opened in South Tottenham. To celebrate, the firm introduced yet another newcomer to its range, 'Silky Teddy', their first artificial silk bear. In 1931 they introduced a range of 'Chubby' bears complete with voice box and also 'Cubby' bears made of fawn plush. In December 1932 the company was registered for the first time as a private limited company. Sadly, Harry Stone died in 1934.

During the 1930s the design of bears evolved; shaved muzzles got longer and bears came in a variety of colours including pink and blue. These proved to be very popular. Another new idea in this period was bears that made growling noises and Chiltern were not slow to offer bears with squeakers and bellows style music boxes.

A new factory was built for the Amersham Works in 1937 but at the outset of the Second World War toy making ceased in Chesham, as both the Waterside and Moor Road factories were required for war work. After the war, all toy-making from Waterside was transferred to the Amersham Works and another new large factory was built near Pontypool in Wales. This was completed in 1947. The Amersham Works continued to make teddy bears and wooden toys, as well as tie and trouser presses. Sadly, production ceased in 1960, when all work was transferred to Wales.

Many of the old-established wooden ware factories continued to make some toys right up until they closed, and they were joined in the early '50s by **Amac Ltd** in Sunnyside House (later called Buck House) in Sunnyside Road, where they made dolls' prams and a variety of other Amacraft toys. However, well before the end of the century, toy manufacturing had ceased in Chesham.

Chapter 12
Utilities

For the first half of the 20th century, Chesham was well served by its own supplies of gas, water and electricity.

The **Chesham Gas & Coke Co** was established in 1846 and their works, at the corner of Waterside and Hospital Hill were completed the following year. Pipes were laid and gas, made from coal in those days, was available to the whole of the town. Street lights were erected first in the High Street, later in the side streets and a lamp lighter was employed.

Above: Chesham gas production workers, and below: the gas showrooms in Upper High Street, 1920s

Other jobs created were involved in manufacturing, sales, installation, and service. Showrooms were initially set up at the works, subsequently moved to Upper High Street and later to Lower High Street. Coke and tar, by-products of the gas making process, were also available for sale at the works.

In 1911 the name was changed to **Chesham and District Gas Co.** but following nationalisation in 1949 the company became part of the Watford Division of Eastern Gas Board. Much rationalisation took place and many local jobs disappeared, although a showroom survived until the 1980s.

The Chesham **Waterworks** had been established in the 1890s and the town had its own municipal surveyor and water inspector. Water was obtained from an artesian well, bored 160 feet into the chalk and lined with cast iron cylinders, with storage in place to hold 200,000 gallons. The facility remained independent until 1973 when it was sold to the Rickmansworth & Uxbridge Valley Water company who had long coveted it. The money received went towards establishing the first Elgiva theatre.

The **Chesham Electric Light & Power Co Ltd** was formed in 1904 and a generating station was established at Higham Mead. Mr R J J Swan, Chief Engineer, oversaw the project to establish the works and the distribution system to most of the town.

In 1920 there was a prolonged battle for the street lighting contract between the Electricity Company and the Gas Company, who had held it for many years. Ultimately the Electricity Company won and the new system took over. Supply was soon extended to Chesham Bois and Berkhamsted. For many years an electricity showroom was maintained in the Broadway. The company remained independent until 1925, when it was taken over by the Metropolitan Electricity Supply Company, **METESCO**.

Following the Electricity Act of 1947 the Company was nationalised and became part of Eastern Electricity, and electricity was supplied from the national grid.

Above: the gas house in Hospital Hill, only recently demolished, and left: Chesham's electricity generating station at Higham Mead

Chesham Electric Light & Power Co lorry, 1920s (courtesy of Chesham Museum)

Chapter 13

Wooden ware

In the middle of the 19th century about 100 men were employed in small-scale wood trades, including shovel-making and bowl turning, largely as cottage industries. By late in the century there were large numbers of turners and other specialists in the new factories. However, some of the smaller craft workshops did not survive long into the 20th century. Others had to adapt their range of products to suit the modern age. Many workers developed into highly skilled craftsmen and ensured the reputation of their employers for high quality goods. Several were family businesses and passed from father to sons.

The availability of timber and the proximity to London also contributed to the importance of Chesham as a centre for the wooden ware trade. However, by the 1930s, high-quality beech trees were becoming scarce locally and timber had to be sourced from further afield.

In an article in *The Bucks Examiner* on 27 March 1937, Mr Bernard Blaser, Clerk to the Council wrote 'nearly every wooden hoop that British children trundle, and nearly every wooden spade they use at the seaside, was made in Chesham. There are five manufacturers of wooden trundle hoops in Great Britain and six of seaside spades, and in each case, all but one are in Chesham'.

After the Second World War there was strong competition from other countries with plentiful timber supplies and cheap labour. By the 1960s many of the family businesses were finished.

Charles Grove had a small-scale business in Waterside, continuing a family tradition of wood turning. He first appeared in *Kelly's Directory* in 1877 but had finished sometime before 1919, when Chiltern Toy Works built a new factory on this site. Mr Grove specialised in making bowling hoops and sieves.

The **Bates** family was involved in the wooden ware business. Robert Bates was a shovel maker in Waterside, at the Minerals, from the 1850s. **Thomas Bates & Sons** were at Bois Saw Mills and in New Road in the late 1890s until some time after 1915. It is believed that Beechwoods (later Beechwood Brushes) took over this Saw Mill in Moor Road (opposite Canada Works) and were there until 1919 when The House of Rees (Leon Rees) took it over and created the Amersham Woodenware and Toy Works. Thomas had started business in Water Lane in the 1860s, but had moved to Church Street by 1891, producing barn and malt shovels.

Grove's wood yard in Waterside (RE)

Shovel-making was a long-established craft in Chesham, for at least the previous 400 years. They were carved from a single plank of wood. Later, Bates were renowned for spades, hoops, yokes, scoops, butchers' trays (for carrying carcasses), bowls, cricket bats and stumps. Thomas' brother Joseph, son of Robert, had been a shovel-maker in Waterside. His son **Joseph Bates**, who started his business in Waterside in the 1890s, later moved to Hivings Hill and Bellingdon Road. Joseph's brother **Parmenas Bates** was in Wey Lane from the early years of the century until his death in the early 1930s. After finishing his education at the British School he went to work for his grandfather, Robert, at The Minerals. He took over this business when Robert died but moved to Wey Lane. He operated from a wood yard there but later built a factory. Among the products made were cricket bats and stumps, hoops and toy spades, barn and malt shovels, bowls and butter prints. Parmenas was at one time a member of Chesham Urban District Council and for many years joint secretary of Chesham Cricket Club. He died aged 75 in 1929 and was buried in Chesham Cemetery.

Four generations of the Bunker family were engaged in the wooden ware trade. **Joseph Bunker** began his business in Germain Street in the 1840s, making general wooden ware and wooden toys. He would walk to London and back for orders, carrying samples of his work with him. He was parish clerk for 50 years, usher of the County Court and one of the first directors of Chesham Building Society. He was also parish constable in sole charge of the lock-up in Church Street. By 1907 the business had moved to Water Lane then Bellingdon Road and finally to Hivings Hill. In the 1930s about 30 people were employed. Timber came from three local woodlands owned by the family. A bungalow was built higher up Hivings Hill from their own timber. In the 1950s some of the firms Joseph originally supplied were still placing orders. By then Bunkers were producing toy cricket bats, (supplied to Woolworth's), hoops, spoons and other domestic ware. Joseph was succeeded by his son Joseph Jr who was succeeded in turn by his son Alfred. Alfred's brother Frederick and Alfred's sons, Dennis and Frank all continued the business. Dennis eventually moved away from the area.

Roland Redding and Frank Bunker were the last directors. Roland was familiarly known as 'Snowball' because of his short white hair. He was a skilled wood turner and it was he who taught Frank, who in later life enjoyed making finely turned lace bobbins as a hobby in his workshop at home. Manufacturing finished at the yard in the early 1960s and the site was leased first to Bilson's Timber Merchants, then around 1989 to Crownform Timber Merchants. They still operate from the site known as Bunker's Yard, providing an efficient and knowledgeable service to the local community. The family believed that their surname derived from the old French name Boncoeur ('good heart') and may have originated from Norman settlers.

Wrights were another family with a long connection to the wooden ware industry. **William Wright**, wooden ware manufacturer, first appears in the commercial directories in 1864 in Church Street. By 1869 he had moved to Water Lane and was operating from the General Saw Mills on the site of an earlier bark mill and tannery. By 1877 the company was known for its cricket bats, trundle hoops, toy spades, sieve hoops, brush boards, spoons, handled and round bowls and butter prints. In the 1881 census William's residence was the nearby Weylands. In 1885 a fire started 'in the timber built and tiled workshop, housing a 12-horsepower

Wright's Wood Yard, Water Lane, 1930s (RE)

steam engine used for sawing timber'. It spread to other buildings and a stack of timber. There was fire and water damage also to the adjoining building, owned by other wooden ware manufacturers Joseph Bunker and George Hawkes. It took 48 pumpers to put the fire out, so presumably no mains water was available. All three properties were owned by Mrs Mary Pegge of Germain Street. By the early 20th century William's sons, William and Thomas, had taken over the business. In the 1890s the factory had been burnt down and rebuilt, but in 1942 another serious fire gutted the new building. There were around 40 employees at this time.

Known locally as Will and Tom, they were well-liked stalwarts of St Mary's Church and by 1947 they had been choristers there for 70 and 63 years – thought at the time to be a national record. They both lived in Wey Lane, William at Holmsdale and Thomas at Weymede. William died in December 1948, aged 79.

The business was taken over by John Pratt, though it didn't survive much longer. It was demolished around 1965.

William Sr's brother **Thomas Wright** started his own business in Waterside, appearing in the directories in 1869 as manufacturer and turner. By 1891 he was listed '& Son', and in 1907 as manufacturers of wooden ware, brushes, barn and malt shovels, cricket bats and stumps, and wood turners.

By 1905 the business was known locally as Jesse Wright's (Thomas' son-in-law) and was advertising as 'English and foreign timber merchant, sawing and planing mills, Berkhampstead Road and Waterside'. They were offering deals, battens and boards 'at London prices' including floor and weatherboards from 4 to 20 feet in length. In addition they were producing 'navvy and garden barrows, field gates, ladders, sheep and bird hurdles and oak sills' as well as providing a service erecting fences.

Jesse Wright was a founder member of Chesham Urban District Council in 1894. The new factory could not have been operating for long at Newtown Mills in the growing industrial suburb when a devastating fire broke out in the engine room on the night of 3rd May 1907. It was the biggest fire in Chesham for many years. Chesham, Berkhamsted and Beaconsfield fire brigades all attended the blaze and the police kept the crowds of

onlookers in hand. The huge brick chimney, a landmark in the area, was cracked near the ground but continued standing. Around £5,000 worth of damage was caused and an estimated 50 tons of timber lost. Around 60 men were employed at the factory at that time and many of them lost their valuable tools in the fire. Some had insurance or belonged to a Benefit Club but most did not. A fund was started to replace them, instigated by Henry Webb, Chairman of Chesham Urban Council and it was expected that £70 would need to be raised.

The fire occurred at a busy time for cricket bats, tennis racquets, etc and a large stock of these was lost. There were large orders in hand but some of them could be started at the Waterside factory.

Eventually the factory was built up again. The power source was a steam engine designed to be coal-fired, though all the waste products were burnt to make it more economical – sawdust, scraps of wood and shavings. Wright's never converted to electricity. The engine drove the whole factory of lathes, band saws and revolving cutters by a complex system of belts running round the building. It took a while to build up enough pressure and it was a full-time

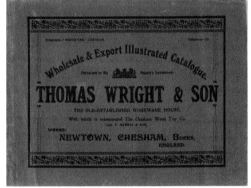

Top, left: William Wright's, c1920, putting finishing touches to wooden wheels; top, middle: the interior of the sawmill; top, right: William Darvell, haulier, with spades for the station from Thomas Wright's; Below: Thomas Wright's first factory in Waterside. Right: Jesse Wright's factory at Berkhampstead Road (RE). Centre: Thomas Wright's catalogue (GN)

Turning polo balls at Thomas Wright's factory

shovel was formed from one plank of wood. Small unusable offcuts of wood were sold by schoolboys as firewood. When the elms were cut down from the avenue in Lowndes Park, they were bought by Wright's and the timber was mostly used for making bowls. Jesse died in 1940, aged 87. He was buried at Chesham Cemetery, workers from the factory lining both sides of the path as the cortege approached. He had been a long-serving deacon at Broadway Baptist Church and his fellow deacons acted as bearers.

The business was carried on by his cousin William Darvell, known as 'Slim' because of his physique. Finally his son Charles took over until the business closed around 1966. The buildings stood empty for some time, then eventually were demolished and the chimney dismantled brick by brick. The site is scheduled to house Chesham's new Healthzone. *Right: Charlie Darvell, as pictured in Thomas Wright's catalogue* (GN)

job for one man to keep the engine in good working order. Condensation had to be drained from the cylinder first thing each morning as any water in the engine could cause it to blow up. It had to be stoked and the shaft bearings lubricated. Any repairs had to be carried out in the evening in order for the engine to be ready for operation the following day.

In the 1930s Jesse built a large family house, known as Springfield House, at the top of what is now Springfield Road, off Waterside. It was approached through timber gates made at the factory and then along a chestnut tree-lined driveway. Some of the land owned there by Jesse Wright was later developed as an industrial estate. Stabling for his horses was at the bottom of Springfield Road, premises later used by Christopher Mulkern for his own plumbing business. This building still stands.

There was a shortage of men during the Second World War and several boys were taken on. Usually boys began at 14 by making chopping boards and by the age of 16 were ready to go on to the band saw. Later they learned to use the circular saw and the plane. There were around 25-30 men employed at this time, including around ten turners. Spoons were a staple product and the Ministry of Defence took many of them. They were made in multiples of two inches in length, from 6-20 inches. About two dozen spoons could be made per day. A bleached product was preferred and this was done by burning sulphur under them in a separate room.

Bomb blocks were a speciality item made during the War, under contract from the Ministry. They were specially designed and shaped to separate mortars and packed in boxes. A few men worked on these exclusively and on overtime.

A well-known worker at Wright's was Fred Harris, a master shovel-maker whose father and grandfather had been engaged in the same occupation. Fred made both malt- and barn-shovels, the latter used for corn, cocoa and coffee beans and during the War for mixing margarine. He worked entirely by hand, using just two tools, a round-edged axe and an adze. Each

Joseph Reynolds ran the factory in Waterside known as Prospect Works from the 1880s, founded in Prospect Terrace by his father, Nathaniel. Another son, Samuel, had previously run it for a few years. A fire completely destroyed the premises; it was rebuilt but moved to a new factory in Waterside in 1888 with a steam saw mill. A William Bates and a Benjamin Grove were among employees who spent all their working lives at Reynolds. Sieve hoops, brush covers, spoons and bowls were among the items the factory specialised in at first, using draw shaves. Yokes and barn shovels were shaped with axes and shaves. A pole lathe was in use for bowl making in the early years of the 20th century, a treadle lathe for ordinary turning. Later a new device was invented, a large wheel, six feet in diameter, turned by hand, and giving increased speed and a better finish. An engine and boiler were eventually purchased, the horse-power gradually being increased over the years.

The company prided itself on being able to supply most small goods required. By this time they were specialising in wooden table-ware, bread boards, bowls, egg cups etc. In the 1940s there were round 35 men employed at the factory. By the 1970s there were 25 men and two women (the first since the early years of the 20th century). Wilfred Reynolds was managing director, with two assistant directors. There was still some piece work available and overtime was allowed. Dust masks were worn by the men, to protect them against the vast amount of sawdust and shavings. The women worked in a sawdust-free room, glueing and hingeing cigar drums and boxes.

By this time electricity was the power source running most of the machines, although there was still some steam and oil used. Transport was by British Road Services; a depot had opened in New Road in 1968. Some products were seasonal, for example gift items were made specifically for the seaside resorts. Other products, such as salad bowls and soap bowls, were made year round. Little stock was kept, so that products were always up-to-the-minute in design, with no outdated items.

Fred Harris using a round edged axe for shovel-making at Wright's (SK)

J Reynolds at a 1950's trade fair (RE)

Much of the wood was imported by this time – box and lignum vitae from the West Indies; mahoganies from Africa; teak from Burma; plywood and veneers from France and Russia and some beech from France. Sycamore, walnut, elm, plane-tree and some beech came from all over Central England and the West Country. Most goods were exported via wholesalers to the United States and Canada, Uruguay, Italy, Austria and Switzerland.

Beech, an expensive light-coloured hard wood, needs to be seasoned out-of-doors before use – it usually was bought in seasoned planks. It was used mostly for shaving bowls and cigarette boxes. Elm, a cheaper soft wood, brown in colour, was dried slowly in a kiln and then used for fruit bowls and cheese boards. Sycamore, a relatively expensive hard white wood, needs careful drying to retain its white appearance in the finished product. It was used extensively for domestic ware such as spoons, bread boards, cheese boards and rolling pins. Mahogany, though expensive, is valued for its rich brown colour and lack of knots. It was often used for fruit bowls and cheese boards. Teak, one of the most expensive woods, needs little drying owing to its oily property. Shrinkage is negligible. Used for bowls and boards, tools had to be of hard steel otherwise the nature of the wood would soon blunt them. Boxwood, very hard and expensive, needs little drying. It creates a very fine dust so workers used masks when sawing. It was usually used for plumbers' tools. Lignum vitae, another very expensive wood, is heavy and one of the hardest woods in the world. It was used for plumbers' tools and bowling balls. Walnut, another hard and expensive wood, the best quality being English, has a grain which makes it particularly appealing for fruit bowls, egg cups, salt and pepper mills in a variety of sizes, table-lamps, bread boards and cheese boards. Chestnut, a very soft wood, is one of the cheapest. It dries quickly and cuts with a clean finish. Very suitable for carving, it was used at Reynolds for butter prints. The firm made garden stakes, fence posts, fruit bowls and church collection-plates from oak. Expensive and very hard, it is one of the longest-growing woods; some grow for hundreds of years before being used. Hickory, with a tight grain, was used for hammer and mallet handles, many other tool handles and drumsticks. Holly, grown locally and fairly inexpensive, with a small diameter, was used for mallets, barrel taps and spigots. Wild cherry, grown locally and very cheap, needed to be dried slowly to prevent cracking. It was used for fancy tableware and some fruit bowls.

One of Reynolds' main products at this time was shaving bowls and lids. These were cut out from kiln-dried planks, cut into widths on a band mill, then planed before being cut into circles on a tubular saw. In the machine shop the insides were turned out on a lathe, then the backs on another. Finally the exterior of the bowls were sanded, also by machine. The lids were turned by hand and the finished product dispatched direct to the soap works where they were filled with shaving soap. Fruit bowls were made in a similar fashion to a rough stage then dried in a kiln for about six weeks before being returned to the turnery department. Here they were fixed to the lathe and turned to the pattern or shape required before being polished inside and out. Salad bowls were also polished whilst still on the lathe but only on the exterior. They were oiled inside. Egg cups were also polished and sometimes were supplied to firms along with stands to hold five or six cups.

All types of mallet were produced, from 'bossing' mallets used by plumbers, to gavels. These were very expensive to make, the head from lignum vitae, the handle from hickory. Turning them was a long process as only a small amount could be turned at one time. Table-lamps, from three to 18 inches high, were another product, made in a variety of patterns. Smaller bedroom lamps were turned from one piece of wood whilst larger lamps required two pieces, a base and an upright. A hole was bored to carry the flex. Standard lamps, made from oak, mahogany or English walnut, were generally five feet six inches in height. The wood had to be well-seasoned to prevent warping of the base, which would throw the upright out of alignment. They were cut on the circular and band saws before going to the turnery department.

Products were of very high quality and were in huge demand, so the future looked good at this stage in the factory's history.

Frederick Leach ran a business in Waterside from the 1920s, on premises originally occupied by the Reed family. In 1881, 65-year-old Job Reed was a wooden ware manufacturer employing six men and Thomas was a sawyer, both in Inkerman Terrace. By 1891 Thomas was listed in *Kelly's Directory* as a wooden ware manufacturer. In the early days they made malt-shovels, sieve rims, butchers' trays, milkmen's yokes, bowls and spoons. By the 1950s they were concentrating on stocks and handles for the brush trade.

Frederick Leach outside his factory c1910 (RE)

Canada Works occupied the former Bois Mill on Amersham Road. This had originally been a water-powered corn mill, converted to steam in 1844. It first appeared in *Kelly's Directory* as Canada Works in 1915, run by Henry John Fox Rose. His father George was miller at Lord's Mill in 1899. Henry changed the name of Bois Mill after visiting Canada. He specialised in building portable houses and poultry houses.

Tommy Hearn took over the business from about 1928 until his death in 1944. The family lived in a house on The Island,

For all kinds of
Portable Houses,
Motor Sheds,
Green Houses,
Garden Lights and
Frames,
Poultry Houses,
Coops and Game
Appliances,
Dog Kennels, &c.,
Apply for list
prices to . .

No. 20.—HOUSE FOR FIELD USE.

H. J. F. ROSE,
CANADA WORKS, CHESHAM.
SATISFACTION GUARANTEED.

next to the works. Tommy's daughter remembers that her father kept chickens and grew vegetables on the plot up to the railway bridge. He had two boats which they used on the Chess. The children played in the woodyard in amongst the sawdust. Wood for the business was seasoned out-side. All types of woodenware were made: gates, chairs, coops, spades, cricket bats, rolling pins, diabalos, fruit bowls. Tommy's daughter used to help pack children's sets of miniature spoons, rolling pins etc into a bowl and label them to sell.

Quite a few local men were employed as wood turners and wood hauliers, including Tommy's brother William Hearn and his nephew Ron Hearn, as they had their own horse and cart to haul the logs. Other employees included Mr Stone, Sid Bristow, Ted Brandon and Ted Burns. Mr Bass looked after the boiler. The men all wore sacking aprons and also folded sacks diagonally into triangles to wear on their heads when it was raining. It would take three or four men to lift the huge logs and push them into the band saw, which Tommy's daughter remembers as being very dirty and noisy. Sid Bristow spent 35 years at the firm, working his way up from boy apprentice to manager. By the early 1950s the firm was a government contractor for

Canada Works, junction of Amersham Road and Moor Road

domestic wood ware and also specialised in tent equipment such as pegs and mallets. 'Props' for theatre and film were made. Various items were made for the Aldershot Tattoo, including dummy guns, pikes, halberds and swords. The company was bought by John Pratt, who later bought William Wright's, but it didn't survive long.

Tommy Hearn at Canada Works (ABE)

James East & Sons Ltd was founded in the 1860s by James East, born 1845, *pictured* (SE). He married Elizabeth Reed, whose father and brother had a wood ware business in Waterside and they had 10 children. James' family had been in Chesham for generations, some of whom had been shovel or hoop makers. His mother, Elizabeth Twitchell, is believed to have descended from the martyr Thomas Harding.

The factory was situated in Albany Place, Broad Street on land purchased by James East and George Webb, brushmaker. This was marshy ground, originally Parrott's Meadows. The river was between the two factories. There was a steam mills at East's, for steaming the bands of beech, ash or oak used to make sieve rims, one of the main products. A row of five cottages was built for the steam mills workers (facing what is now Albany car park). A family house, No 24 Broad Street, was built, which is still in the family today. Originally there were stables and an orchard and the land extended back to Bellingdon Road. In the 1960s this was compulsorily purchased by the Council for the Albany Place car park.

In the 1880s, the Metropolitan railway was being constructed, and James East's company won the contract for making the fence posts. Posts were taken up by horse and cart to where the cutting was being constructed and they returned with trees cut down where the line was being laid. This was probably as far as Harrow-on-the Hill and became such a regular trip the horse would know its own way home. Fencing was also supplied for the gardens of the new houses in the area.

In the early years of the 20th century the factory was almost the sole supplier of wooden ware to Smithfield Market. Butchers' blocks in particular were made, around 30 at a time being sent by horse-drawn carriage. In 1890 a 20 inch butcher's block was priced at eight shillings. By the 1970s the price was £20. Other items were gambals, used for hanging the slaughtered animals, and shoulder trays, used to carry a whole sheep or pig. These trays were made by hand from ash imported from Canada. Each tray required half a tree and as many as 30 trees could be deposited in the yard at a time. The BBC borrowed a tray for their 1970s production of *Oliver Twist*, as they had been unable to locate one anywhere else. Yokes were made, from beech or ash, which were used for carrying pails of milk, or sent to the West Country, where they were used for carrying shrimps. Wheelbarrows with wooden wheels and toy spades were also made.

East's wood yard c1905, with James East, far right (SK)

Cyril Sanders, grandson of James East, with his own grandson Peter Evans, pictured at East's in 1981 (RE)

Barn and malt shovels were another speciality of the factory. Barn shovels were mainly used for corn. Malt shovels, for brewers, were made up to 16 inch wide from beech or poplar. A wedge shape was cut out of the tree, which was then finished by hand. Shovels were sent to the plantations in Burma for shovelling tea and coffee when drying. Several different tools were used for forming the shovels. Employees were required to purchase their own tools and had them made by local blacksmiths. Bill Moulder was a well-known local man who made shovels. He had learned the trade at East's from leaving school at 14, apprenticed to his father. His brothers Jesse and Joe also worked for the company. Their grandfather and great-grandfather had also been involved in the wood trade.

Sieve rims were made from strips, mainly of beech, sometimes ash or oak, steamed in a steam box until pliable to be bent into shape. Several sizes of cooks' and garden sieves were made. These would then be taken up to London for wireworkers to insert the wire mesh. Employees first learned circular and band sawing and made simple items like spoons and toy spades. Later, as top craftsmen, they could earn 25 shillings per week, working from 6.30am to 6.30pm weekdays, until 2pm on Saturdays. During the summer months, after a half-hour break, they were required to walk up to the Vale, where the horses were kept, and work there on haymaking until 10.30pm. Pole lathes were used for turning items, the wood turned wet so it wouldn't split. Items were then put in the drying shed, which was open so the wind could blow through. There could be eight to ten trees arriving on a pole trailer, which had to negotiate the narrow Parrott's Path to access the factory.

James died in 1925 and his four sons took over the business for a short time, but one left and another died young. James' daughter Florence had married Arthur Edward Sanders. It was their son, Cyril, who took over the company in the 1930s and formed a limited company. During the Second World War shovels were produced for the armaments industry as wooden shovels produced no sparks when shovelling ammunition. Around this time there was a serious fire at the factory and everything was lost but the business was built up again from scratch.

Another of James' grandsons, his son Thomas' son Leslie, grew up near the woodyard. He helped look after the horses and continued to do this and work in the factory after he left school at the age of 14. There was little work left after the Second World War. The factory was left empty for some time. By the 1950s and 1960s timber was scarce locally and beech was brought from Kent, Sussex and as far away as Shropshire. There could be eight to ten trees arriving on a pole trailer, which had to negotiate the narrow Parrott's Path to access the factory.

In the early 1960s William Wright's wooden ware factory was in decline and one of their workers approached Cyril Sanders with the suggestion of using East's factory. Eight workers moved there, taking some of their machinery and an associate company was formed, Cheston Woodware Ltd. They had wanted to name it Chesswood but there was already a company in existence with this name. They concentrated on small domestic items, some for Smithfields and Billingsgate, eg elm fishboards.

Sieve rims were still being made and around this time a contract was made with Woolworths, whose Head Office was in Cardiff, to supply them with garden sieves. These were mainly 18 inches in diameter and were packed in lots of six. Cooks' sieves were made for a London company, who collected them from the factory, 40 or 50 dozen at a time. These were 5 to 12 inches in diameter. Bowling hoops, spoons and rolling pins were also made.

By the early 1960s plastic was taking over from wood. During Harold Wilson's government, health & safety regulations dictated that no wooden chopping boards or wooden-handled knives could be used by the meat and fish industries. Schools could not use wooden spoons or boards as plastic was considered more hygienic. This had a huge impact on the wooden ware factories and employee numbers dwindled significantly. Schools all over the country had been supplied with these items. There had also been a huge demand for towel rollers, in particular from the Co-op but even these were affected by the new regulations. Cheston is still in operation though in a very limited way.

Frederick East was a cousin to James East. He ran a business in Townsend Road, with a saw mill, started by his father Ebenezer, wood turner in the late 1860s. Ebenezer had been a bowl and shovel maker in the 1840s in the High Street as were his brothers Daniel and Nathaniel who were also hoop renders

In addition Ebenezer was a beer retailer and by 1847 was at the Three Tuns public house in White Hill, where he continued until at least 1877. Here he had a pit saw in the middle of the road, requiring traffic to negotiate a way around it. Daniel moved to Waterside where he made hoops. Nathaniel was still in the High

Street in 1869. Frederick's son, also Frederick, continued the business in Townsend Road until the 1950s. Some of the items they produced were sieve rims, broomstick handles and tent poles. The site was taken over by Beechy Bucks Products.

Sundt Woodware Ltd had its origins in Samuel Treacher's 17th century foundry producing wooden spokes and wheels. At some point a Treacher probably married into the Webb family as by the 1840s a Treacher Webb was a turner, making bowls, spoons and shovels. A factory was started in Newtown and products included stock handles and butter prints. Late in the century Treacher moved to Alexander Street and his sons came into the business. In 1898 Norwegian Finn Sundt arrived in England and imported Norwegian goods. With the outbreak of the First World War he joined forces with Webb's and ran the business with around 50 men and boys. They supplied broom handles to the services and also produced handles for pick axes and shovels using local timber.

After the war, Sundt returned to importing for a while before developing new products for the company, including coat hangers, rolling pins and other domestic items. During the Second World War various types of brush handles were produced for the Ministry of Supply, also tent poles.

Sundt's Cameron Road premises (RE)

With the 1950s came modernisation and a decision to specialise in brush handles for the domestic kitchen. These handles were supplied to Kleeneze, Betterwear, Prestige and Addis. By the end of the decade a unique method of covering wood and metal with plastic had been developed and in 1960 a new factory was opened in Cameron Road. Timber was by this time imported from Brazil and the Far East. It was transported by sea to Sundt's storage facility in London where it was weathered for six months and arrived at the factory in various sizes ready for the machines.

As time went by there was a change of emphasis as the older wooden products were phased out and were replaced by plastic variants. A dedicated plastics division, Sundt Plastics, was set up with full injection moulding capabilities. At the peak of production there were around 140 employees at the factory, many of whom were the third generation of the same family. Three million broom handles were produced each year.

In 1963 the company was bought by the Kleeneze Group. In 1985 it was decided to transfer operations to its headquarters in Bristol as a cost-saving measure. There were around 25 employees left when the factory closed, many of whom were approaching retirement age.

Frederick East's old and new factories, c1935 (RE)

Howard Brothers continued another family tradition. Joseph (Joe) and John Rose Howard were the sons of Joseph Liberty Howard, a carpenter. He was the subject of one of the first major operations at the Cottage Hospital when he had his leg amputated after a cricketing injury, aged 22. He evidently had a rather macabre sense of humour as he later kept his preserved and polished tibia and fibula bones standing in a corner of the office at the Howard Brothers' works. He fashioned his own crutches and also selected and stored elm boards for his own coffin throughout his working life.

The brothers' business, known as the Steam Works, began in the High Street, (where the Town Hall is now situated), continuing from their uncle James who had been a wooden ware manufacturer, carver and general turner, specialising in butter prints. Business grew and the site became too small. Around 1920 they moved to premises in Chilton Avenue, near to the Nashleigh Arms. The factory was known as the Avenue Works, derived from the avenue of trees running from the back of the premises to Addison Road. A power sawbench was used. Timber trunks were first sawn into manageable lengths then laid on a huge trolley which ran on rails into the sawing shed. Here was a fixed power-driven cross-cut saw. The trolley was slowly winched onto the reciprocating saw blade and was gradually rendered down into planks which were then cut into smaller sections. These were turned into a variety of small domestic wooden ware items.

Before the Second World War demand from all over the world kept five master carvers fully employed in producing the butter prints for which the company was renowned. The war years and the butter shortage reduced demand until there was only enough work for two carvers. One was Ken Whittle. He served a seven-year apprenticeship and spent the rest of his working life forming butter prints and moulds and shortbread moulds by 'reverse' or 'sunk' carving. Some of the products he made were ordered by royalty, the BBC and major airline companies.

Family crests, coats of arms, initials, monograms and cyphers were in demand. Sizes varied from small prints for stamping butter pats for table use, to display moulds for exhibitions.

Butter prints were among the earliest trade marks and at one time each county would have had its own pattern, often derived from a classical design. In addition there were common designs such as the rose and thistle, pineapple, star, shell, wheat sheaf, strawberry, swan, cow and flowers.

Above: the Howard family. Below: The trolley bringing timber trunks into the works. Right: Mr Lawrence, one of the carvers at Howard's (BH)

Ken Whittle, master craftsman at Howard's (RE)

Oblong prints were supplied by Howard's in three sizes, usually carved with flower, thistle, acorn, swan, strawberry or cow designs. Roller prints were carved with floral or thistle designs. Butter moulds, in four sizes, had swan, pineapple, sheaf, dolphin, hen and chick, or squirrel. A small mould for table use was popular with the American market. Sycamore was mostly used for prints and moulds but boxwood, a harder and closer-grained wood, was used for very intricate designs. Ken Whittle was celebrated locally in December 1960 when he appeared on the popular BBC quiz game *What's My Line?* and beat the panel.

John Rose Howard was a shrewd and highly respected businessman, but was appreciated too for his great sense of humour. He was a staunch Baptist and was instrumental, together with his brother Joseph, in encouraging a move from Townfield Yard to the developing Newtown, where a new church was built in 1927. He died in 1941 and was buried in Chesham Cemetery.

The Howard brothers had an older brother, William George, whose son Jack joined the firm on leaving school at 14. He served a full apprenticeship, learning all aspects of the trade, becoming a carver, turner and general woodworker. He went into the managerial side of the company and eventually took over as managing director. There were around 50 employees at the peak of production but sadly the business gradually declined until it closed in 1976 owing to a lack of skilled labour.

An auction was held by London auctioneers Henry Butcher & Co in February of that year when all the woodworking machinery, timber, plant and equipment was sold in lots. The premises remained empty for some period after that. They were subject to

The avenue of trees at Addison Road which gave its name to the Howard Brothers' Avenue Works (BH)

increasing vandalism, culminating in a serious fire. The buildings were eventually demolished and the site sold for re-development. It is now occupied by the Howard Industrial Estate.

The **General Woodworking Co** was a subsidiary company of Brandon's furniture store and in the 1920s and '30s was located behind what is now Chittenden's electrical shop in The Broadway. One of the interesting items they made was a Perfecta Trouser Press. This was designed, developed and patented by Herbert Edmunds of Blucher Street whilst working for them. The company was eventually taken over by Marmet of Letchworth. Also in the 1930s Bellingdon Road was home to **Chesham Sawmills** run by Mr E Fitzgerald on a large site opposite the cemetery lodge. 20 years later, **Woodpecker Ltd**, run by Messrs Seymour and West, was making wooden ware close to this site.

Fitzgerald's of Chesham Sawmills at Bellingdon Road, c1920 (RE)
Below: receipt dated 1922 (SK)

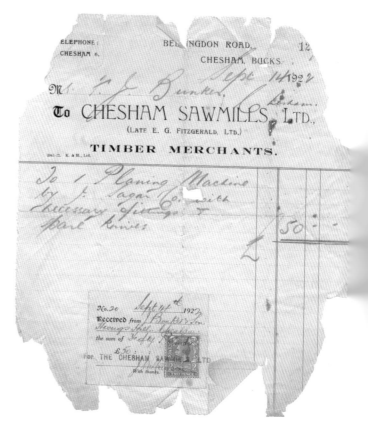

Wooden ware tools and techniques from James East's

Stuart King, a local historian and craftsman, is an avid collector of old tools. He set about making a permanent record of Chesham's wooden ware industry, with many tools and products gleaned from the workshops of James East at Albany Place, before demolition in 1984. He also interviewed the director, Cyril Sanders, then aged 90 years. The tools are now on display at the Chesham Wooden Ware Collection at Chiltern Open Air Museum.

Tools used by Jesse Moulder –
a lathe-maker's froe and Chesham-made bill

Using an adze in shovel-making

Bentware – a child's trundle hoop; a half-gallon elm measure;
a sieve and unused bends

Using a hollow shave in shovel-making

The Chesham Wooden Ware Collection at Chiltern Open Air Museum.
Note the 8-foot-long baker's peel for reaching loaves at the back of the oven

The wood bending shop

Chapter 14
Specialist manufacturing

Adhesive products

Brian Jeays Wardle had lived in Buckinghamshire since 1955, and in 1961 started his own company in Chesham. He had been involved with industrial adhesives with Dunlop Special Products and had risen to the position of Industrial Sales Manager but had become disillusioned and wanted his own business. He found a plot of land in Moor Road and with an investment of £5000 and a handful of employees, **Industrial Adhesives Ltd** was born. After some early setbacks the business took off, more land was purchased and new buildings erected. The adhesives range included water-based, hot melt and solvent/cement products. With an active development and applications laboratory new variants were frequently introduced. All went well until 1976 when the factory was struck by a series of fires. The most serious of these occurred in the early hours of June 2nd and resulted in an explosion in the solvent production area which produced about half the company's output. Several buildings had to be replaced and it was a year before full production was achieved again.

In 1981 Mr Wardle sold the business to Burmah Castrol but remained for a year as Managing Director until his retirement. Burmah had taken a strategic decision to build a new division based on adhesives. However this proved to be difficult and in 1998 they sold the business on to H B Fuller (UK) Ltd, the British subsidiary of an American company. The business survived until the end of the century but was closed early in the 21st century when all work was transferred to other Fuller factories in the North of England and in Germany. At its peak the company provided over 120 jobs in Chesham.

Two other companies involved with adhesive products were in Chesham in the latter part of the 20th century. **Kwikstik Products Ltd**, later to become **DRG Kwikseal Products,** made sealing and bonding products mainly based on self-adhesive tapes. Their head office was in Mineral Lane and they also had three factories in the town. The company moved to Dunstable in 1984. **Chiltern Adhesive Product Supplies,** from their premises in Reynolds Yard, Waterside, were distributing and converting self-adhesive tapes, foams, sealants and fastening systems.

Industrial Adhesives headquarters in Moor Road; recently demolished to make way for the Chess Business Park

Aircraft seats

Seats for aircraft have been made in Chesham for over 50 years. It started when Mr Norman Riley set up a factory in Severalls Avenue for, but independent from, the American company **Flight Equipment and Engineering Ltd** (**FEEL**).

Early success was achieved with the 'Payloader' seat. It was a double passenger seat designed to fold up against the fuselage to make way for cargo whenever required. A second factory and offices were opened in Asheridge Road and the business flourished, with major contracts with BEA and many of the world's

major airlines. A luxurious Flight Equipment seat was supplied to King Hussein of Jordan for his private charter jet.

Long before the legal requirements for dynamic testing were introduced, Flight Equipment built a test-run down the steep slope at the side of the Asheridge Road factory, where seats could be released on a sled and crashed into a block to simulate a crash.

In the mid 1970s, John Tcheng became Managing Director and the company began a period of rapid expansion.

Advertisement from the 1950s

There were many innovations, with some of the first CNC milling machines in the area being installed.

The company also introduced an innovative style of composite seat back, which provided economy class passengers with more comfort and more legroom. This style of back has now been adopted by most aircraft seat builders around the world. During the 1980s the company grew rapidly and moved to premises in Nashleigh Hill on the site of the old foundry owned by Frederick Kay. Well over 100 people were employed at the peak with developed skills in engineering design and fabrication, plastics technology and upholstery.

The growth of the company subsequently brought about the end of seat production. It was taken over by an American Company, BE Aerospace, who moved the operation to larger premises in Leighton Buzzard, but a few years later all seat manufacture was transferred to Ireland and the United States.

Another aircraft seat manufacturer was created in the town when Mr Ted Burne left FEEL in 1956 to set up **Flying Service Engineering and Equipment Ltd.** Like FEEL, their business developed with orders from airlines and airforces all over the world. In the 1980s and to this day, most manufacturers' seat frames had two horizontal aluminium tubes supported on front and rear legs;

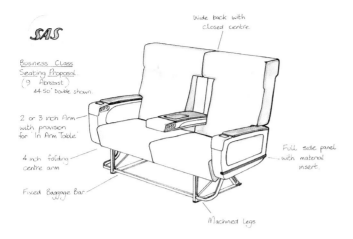

Proposed Flight Equipment seat design for SAS, 1980s (GO)

Ted and his team designed a seat with single legs and horizontal tubes, which provided far more leg room and reduced the risk of broken legs in the unlikely event of an accident. On the basis of this unique design they received major contracts from Laker Airways, British Caledonian and, later, a significant order from British Airways for the economy seating of the majority of its fleet, which is still being supported today. In common with most other aircraft seat manufacturers, the company has developed seating to meet the current dynamic seat requirements. At its peak the company employed some 350 staff and is still family owned, operating from two sites in Chesham with another factory in Wales.

Aluminium foil and packaging

Green Polyfoil Papers came to Chesham from Wembley in the mid-1960s and moved into a small factory on the northern side of Asheridge Road. The Aluminium Company of Canada (Alcan) had just purchased Green PP's foil supplier Fisher Foils of Wembley and, as part of a vertical integration programme, they also purchased Green PP and renamed it **Alcan Polyfoil Ltd**. With the business expanding it wasn't long before they moved over the road to the 'Garden Factory' previously occupied by George Williams Co Ltd and then Van Houten. At this time there were two main product lines, coloured foil Christmas decorations and the recently introduced but growing 'cooking foil'. Bulk rolls of aluminium foil from the Alcan Foil rolling mills in Wembley were broken down and wound, originally using hand operated machines, on to cardboard tubes in short lengths for domestic use. New machines, flow lines and automated equipment were added and production and sales greatly increased by the end of the decade.

By this time the demand for aluminium

Aluminium food container press (BD)

foil containers for the food industry was increasing and a new division, **Alcan Ecko Ltd,** was formed to handle this business as the result of a joint venture with Ecko Products of Chicago. This new division shared the Asheridge Road site with Alcan Polyfoil Ltd.

In the early 1970s a new warehouse and press shop were built to accommodate the expanding business. These were opened at a grand ceremony by the Rt Hon Clement Freud MP, the mayor and town councillors in November 1973, pictured below (BD).

In the late '70s Alcan Polyfoil left Chesham for a new site in Raans Road, Amersham, but the foil packaging business continued to grow and two more warehouses were built and new press shops were added. By this time Alcan Ecko had become recognised as a world leader in aluminium foil container manufacturing.

In 1994 the business was taken over by a consortium of financial institutions via financial backing to selected members of the management team and the name was changed to **Ecko Packaging Ltd.** At the peak of its activities the business employed 300 people on the Asheridge Road site but began to decline from the time of the management buy-out. In 2001 the company was taken over again and left the town in 2005.

Christmas decorations and lighting

For many years now at Christmas time, the streets of most British cities have been brightened by lights and decorations. During the 1960s it is more than likely that these were made in Chesham by **Chrysaline Ltd.** The company came to Chesham from Berkhamsted in 1960 and employed 50 people at its Waterside factory, opposite Shackman's. The company also made domestic lighting, electrical equipment and lampshades. However, the recession of the late 1960s hit shopping at Christmas and the lights went out in London's Oxford Street in 1967 and shortly afterwards in Regent Street. This affected Chrysaline, who left Chesham in 1969.

Right: a Chrysaline decoration, illustrated by Madeleine Fletcher

Coconut matting

Mat weaving in Bois Moor Road (RE)

The London Mat & Matting Company opened in Chesham at the start of the 20th century at the Old Crown Works in Bois Moor Road. This was later called Montagu Mills and the proprietor was Edmund Vine who lived in Stanley Avenue. The company made mats and matting by weaving the fibres or coir from the husks of coconuts. Later they also sold Axminster and Wilton carpets and rugs, rubber mats, and cord rugs and mats.

In the late 1940s the business was taken over by A W Cooke but managed by C S Harrison Ltd of High Wycombe. Subsequently, in the 1960s, it was sold to a Mr Bodigian who ran the London Carpet Company, also in High Wycombe. He consolidated his wholesale carpet business at the Chesham site and began importing coconut matting from India as production at Chesham was phased out. In 1974 the Chesham works closed and the business moved to Thame where it is still operating.

Electronic valves and lamps

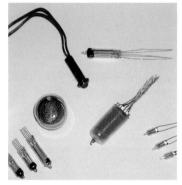

In the late 1920s Mr De Laszlo started The High Vacuum Valve Company, with a factory in Farringdon Road, London, manufacturing specialised thermionic valves. In 1939 Mr Laszlo and his wife were killed in a car accident and the company faced the prospect of closure. However, the sales manager, Harry Diggle, persuaded the Automatic Telephone and Electric Co of Liverpool to take over the company and it was re-named **Hivac Ltd**. With the onset of the Second World War it was decided to move the factory out of London and it was set up in Harrow.

Miniature valves were of considerable interest to the armed forces and the Ministry of Supply built the Chesham factory in Asheridge Road for Hivac to manufacture fuse valves for use in anti-aircraft shells. These valves had to be very rugged to withstand the force of firing and were used in a special circuit, so that the shell exploded at its nearest point to the target aircraft. The gunners only had to aim and fire, setting the fuse was unnecessary. Manufacture of these fuse valves continued at Chesham until after the Korean war. The Harrow factory made special valves for the navy, but this too was very secret work and most of Hivac's workers had no idea what the products were used for.

In the early 1950s the Harrow factory was closed and work transferred to a specially designed factory at Ruislip which included a super clean area for the production of '"Reliable Pack Set Valves'. Over the next ten years this factory expanded considerably, especially with the production of cold cathode tubes and then

Hivac staff dinner, 1945

Hivac's Asheridge Road factory

neon indicators. The Chesham factory also expanded and when production of fuse valves ceased, the manufacture of neon indicators was transferred to Chesham. Much of this work involved careful manual assembly and to assist in this work a large force of out-workers was employed. At its peak they numbered over 70.

AT&E, and also Ericsson in Nottingham, were taken over by the Plessey Co, and for some years Hivac operated as a division of Plessey and took over the valve division of Ericsson. However with the development of transistors the demand for valves gradually decreased and work then concentrated on lamps and indicators. Following another takeover, this time by General Instruments of America (GIA), the Ruislip factory was closed and all work transferred to Chesham in 1972. At this time the workforce totalled over 600.

Gradually demand for filamentary lamps and cold cathode tubes declined and the Chesham factory closed in 1989 when all neon indicator production was transferred to another GIA factory in Suffolk.

Hivac miniature lamp assembly (LC)

Flags and banners

It was in 1837 that **George Tutill** started making flags and banners at a small factory in Islington. At the end of the 1830s he moved everything to 83 City Road, London where the factory remained for the next 100 years. In the early 1890s the firm opened a small branch factory in Bellingdon Road, Chesham. A year or two later they moved to the old silk mill in Waterside (later the Royal Bucks Laundry) where they remained until the 1920s when they relocated to Higham Road to be near to the river which was important for removing the excess inks used in flag making by hand washing.

In 1941 the London branch was bombed out and all departments, with the exception of the studio at Hitchin, were moved to Chesham.

Flags were made of woven or knitted fabric to allow the wind to pass through. The patterns on the flags were either sewn with coloured silks or hand painted. Later the patterns were printed. By the end of the century the company was also making eyelet-holed, PVC advertising banners in any required size.

In the early part of the 20th century the company had close links with the Trades Union movement for who many large hand painted banners were made. The banners would typically depict the benefits that would accrue from union membership, the dignity of the trade, brotherhood, unity and justice.

Special and royal occasions have invariably brought special orders to the company. For the coronation of George VI in 1937 George Tutill Ltd made a Union Jack 60 feet long and 50 feet wide. A workforce of about 20 people continues to maintain the company's position as one of the country's largest manufacturers of flags, flagstaffs, banners and pennants.

Tutill's Higham Road factory

A Tutill trade union banner (courtesy of The People's History Museum, Manchester)

Gas and oil boilers

Kayenco industrial boilers (BK)

Just after the Second World War, Frederick Kay started a business in a converted stable in Kings Cross, London. Four years later, in 1949, **Frederick Kay (Engineering) Ltd** moved to Chesham and settled on a site in Nashleigh Hill, where they specialised in the design, development and manufacture of industrial and domestic boilers. In 1951 the company developed a new range of domestic boilers which pioneered the use of welded fabrications rather than the orthodox heavy castings used previously. These boilers formed the 'Kayenco' range. In the same year the company also pioneered a new type of flame failure protection device which added considerably to boiler safety.

As a result of this early work Frederick Kay Ltd were among the first boiler manufacturers to produce a clean, attractive and well designed boiler which was an original specification and not a converted solid fuel appliance.

As time went on, the name 'Kayenco' became well known in many parts of the world. Expansion continued throughout the 1950s with the emphasis shifting to large industrial boilers. Employment was provided for about 100 workers, including skilled welders and sheet metal workers and trained sales and service engineers. A full apprenticeship scheme was in place for young workers.

In 1960 the company became a partner of the Allied Ironfounders Ltd organisation (AIL) and five years later was taken over completely. At this point Frederick's son Brian left the organisation and, with his wife Angela, started **Kayanson Engineers Ltd,** operating from an office in Chesham High Street. By 1966 a new range of boilers had been designed and manufacture was started in Lydney in Gloucestershire. The product range was continually developed with special designs for waste heat, and sludge gas units for fuel saving and greater efficiency. A presence was maintained in Chesham until 2002 when Kayanson Engineers Ltd merged with the Hoval Group. Sadly, production at the Nashleigh Hill factory had ceased over 30 years earlier.

Hair products

In 1907 Eugene Schueller, a young chemist, created the first synthetic hair dye which he called 'Aureole'. Two years later he started the Societe Francais de Tentures Inoffensives Pour Cheveux (The Safe Hair Dye Company of France). This later became L'Oreal.

In 1932 Mr H S Laurenson founded **Golden Ltd** with the rights to manufacture and sell L'Oreal products to hairdressing salons in the UK. Like many other companies they moved to Chesham early in the Second World War and in 1941 were based in a house in Springfield Road. Later they moved into the Empire Works in Station Road and in the early 1950s, when the business really took off, they moved again to a larger factory in Higham Road. At one time Golden Ltd employed 300 people, including a sales force of 60.

In 1968, L'Oreal, by now the world's largest cosmetics company, purchased a major stake in Golden Ltd and moved much of the manufacturing work to a new factory in Leighton Buzzard. However work continued with much research and development being undertaken in the associated Laudale Laboratories.

By the late 1970s the site was occupied by **Parim (Lancome) Ltd**, another subsidiary of L'Oreal, who remained in Chesham until the end of the century.

Golden's factory, Higham Road

Jewellery and instruments

D Shackman and Sons was started in London in 1904, making rings and fine jewellery. In the late 1930s the firm also started an instrument division. With the advent of the Second World War the company moved to Chesham and in 1940 were housed in part of the Carlton Press premises in the Broadway. They were immediately engaged in making optical measuring instruments and lenses for the war effort. In 1943 the company moved to Waterside where they stayed until 1981. At this time they were also involved in converting original gold currency, brought out of Germany by fleeing Jews, into jewellery. After the war Shackman's continued to

Shackman's Chiltern Works, Waterside

Cover of a Shackman's camera brochure (BD)

Ladies' handbags

Chesham had long been involved in the working of leather, through boot and shoe manufacture, but in 1919 a new company moved in to make ladies' handbags. Shillaker's was formed in 1902 in the City of London by brothers William and Edgar Shillaker, where they made leather belts, and in 1908 they formed **W Shillaker's & Co Ltd.**

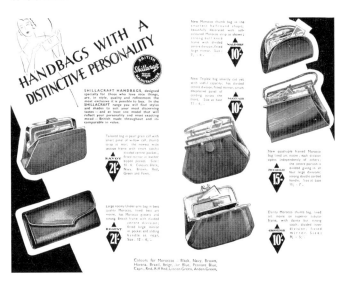

Below; Shillaker's packing department (DH)

make watch cases and integrated bracelets as well as other pieces of bespoke jewellery. The instrument business continued to develop and additional premises were taken in Mineral Lane. Here they made gun dial sights, sextants and gap measures for military use and also specialist high speed cameras and document copying apparatus. The first flight recorders for the Comet airliners were made by D Shackman and Sons.

In 1953 a powder box made in platinum by Shackman's *(pictured)* was presented to the Queen at the Metallurgists Metals exhibition.

For many years the business was run by David Shackman's sons Reuben and Albert, who were greatly respected by the staff. At its peak the business employed 200 people locally, many of whom were highly skilled and stayed with the company for many years. After the jewellery business closed, the instrument division continued to give work to about 50 employees until 1993, when it was purchased by Anamax.

As the science of electronics developed in the second half of the century, a vast number of instrument companies sprang up nationwide and several of these came to Chesham. By the 1970s, **G H S Electronics Ltd** were established in Severalls Avenue. Run by George Howard-Sorrell, a car enthusiast who drove in the Monte Carlo rally, they made transformers, filters, power supplies and medical electronic instruments. By the mid '80s, **Texscan Instruments Ltd** had moved into the town from Berkhamsted to make broad band amplifiers at their facility in Watermeadow.

Meanwhile, at the other end of town, **Sensonics Ltd** were making condition monitoring equipment on the site of the old Britannia boot works in Addison Road. They had been based in Chartridge from 1974 but left the town in 1997 with the loss of 42 jobs when the business was sold by the owners Peter Brotherhood Ltd. By the end of the century the Chiltern works in Waterside was occupied by **Sundance Multiprocessor Technology Ltd** who are employed in the design, manufacture and sale of digital signal processing software and equipment.

Sensonics' factory

In 1919 the brothers were joined by Maurice Heistercamp who had fled from Belgium with his wife and baby son during the First World War. He became manager, and introduced ladies' leather handbag manufacture. After the war, larger premises were required and the company decided to move to Chesham for several reasons: the good rail service to London, the existing leather goods industry in the town and the known skills of local ladies engaged in lace making.

Alma Road was the chosen site, opposite a boot factory, and ten people were employed in premises built by Rust & Ratcliffe. In 1921 Maurice decided to return to Belgium to set up his own business and his place was taken by his younger brother Camille. A further extension was built in 1925, by which time the company was employing 50 people, mostly women. It was a very desirable place to work and always had a waiting list for employment.

During the early 1930s the trade name 'Shillacraft' was adopted. Bags were sold to leading stores including Harrods, Selfridges and Dickens & Jones. Mass production methods were introduced, sales and output increased, and by 1939 there were 125 employees producing 4,000 to 5,000 handbags per week.

The company exhibited regularly at the annual British Industries Fair and customers included Queen Mary and other members of the Royal Family.

With the onset of the Second World War, handbag manufacture ceased and the factory was taken over, under the direction of the Admiralty, by the Telegraph Condenser Company (TCC). Machinery was moved into storage, although some manufacturing of gas mask cases and shopping bags continued in a small factory in How's Yard off Berkhampstead Road.

In 1958 Camille bought out the Shillaker family interest in the company and went into partnership with Jane Shilton of London. In 1961, on retirement, Camille sold his shares to Alex Shilton and Shillaker's became a subsidiary of Shilton Ltd. In 1981 it was decided not to renew the Alma Road lease, so the Chesham facility closed and all manufacturing transferred to Shilton's new factory in Fulham. 60 factory employees and 25 home-based leather workers lost their jobs.

Medical equipment

Established in London in 1770 by George Carsberg, **H G Carsberg & Son,** manufacturers of surgical and anaesthetic instruments and apparatus, came to Chesham in 1938. Originally located in Severalls Avenue, the company moved into the old Chiltern Toy works in Waterside in 1942.

After the war the firm moved to a purpose built factory in Asheridge Road. All instruments were entirely British made and supplied to many eminent surgeons, who collaborated on the design and development. Close relationships were also established with metallurgists and engineers to ensure maximum product efficiency, safety and durability. The wide product range included copper and brass dilators, silver and stainless steel bougies and tissue tolerant silver tracheotomy tubes.

At one time the company employed 90 people and became the largest manufacturer of non-ferrous surgical instruments in the UK. They also made instruments for dental and veterinary work.

In 1970 the company merged with Froud & Sons Ltd to become **C&F Surgical Instruments,** but left Chesham in 1976 when taken over by Downs Surgical Instruments and moved to Braintree. It is now part of Smith's Industries.

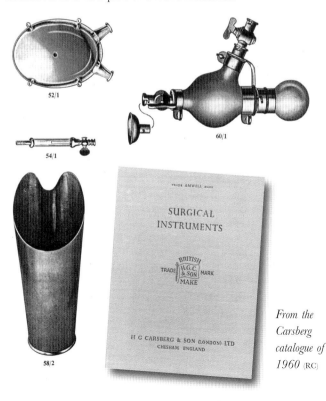

From the Carsberg catalogue of 1960 (RC)

Another medical equipment company came to Chesham in 1963. **Blease Anaesthetic Equipment Ltd** owed much to the energy and enthusiasm of its founder John Blease, who before the Second World War, had built a reputation in tuning motorcycle engines. His wartime experience in British Hospitals acquainted him with the use of 'iron lungs' in the treatment of polio victims and the speciality of anaesthesia. In 1944 he set up his company in Liverpool to design and manufacture electrically-driven lung ventilators.

The company later moved to Northwood Hills before finally settling in Chesham at Deansway. Just before this time Dr Roger Manley joined the company. In 1961, whilst working as anaesthetics research registrar at Westminster Hospital, Manley designed a machine to monitor or assist breathing during anaesthesia or other forms of unconsciousness.

Blease ventilator production line, 1964 (ES)

This invention changed his career. Having switched to engineering he became technical director of Blease and two years later was appointed managing director. He was also a director of Hutchinson Engineering, a precision engineering company, started in 1956 by Harold Hutchinson, which took over Blease in 1963 to become, for a few years, **Hutchinson Blease Ltd,** and later **Blease Medical Ltd**. The Blease Manley Ventilator was an immediate and lasting success with continuing improvements and modifications. *Pictured below: Series 5050 Pulmoflator, 1960s* (SMA).

However through the 1970s and 1980s few new products were introduced and the company became a smaller player in the anaesthesia market. Fortunately new products in the '90s signalled a recovery in their market position and in 1993 the sales, marketing and service departments moved to new premises in Asheridge Road and a new purpose built vaporiser production area was developed at the Deansway facility. By the end of the century more than 70 percent of output was exported, leading to the company receiving a Queen's Award for Export in 1997. Also Blease were awarded the Queen's Award for Enterprise, innovation category, for the 8500 anaesthesia ventilator. At one time local employees numbered 150.

Briefly in the 1970s another company, **BOC Medishield**, making similar equipment to Blease, were located in Springfield Road. This was as a result of collaboration between the British Oxygen Company (BOC) and Dr Manley, who by this time had parted company with Blease.

Mixing equipment

Silverson Machines Ltd was founded in 1946, based originally in London, at Battersea. In 1969 they moved to the site in Waterside previously occupied by Chrysaline Ltd, closing operations in Battersea sometime afterwards. They are still operating.

Silverson is a world leader in the design and manufacture of high shear mixers, used in industries as diverse as chemicals, food, pharmaceuticals, cosmetics and petrochemicals. Mechanical and electrical engineers are employed in designing and manufacturing mixers for blending, emulsifying, homogenising, disintegrating and dissolving. The company offers a wide range of equipment, from small laboratory scale mixers for volumes as little as one millilitre, up to 300,000 litre disintegrator systems.

Special designs to meet specific customer requirements are also offered. All these are wholly manufactured on-site in Chesham and exported to customers in over 150 countries.

Top: The Silverson offices and factory in Waterside.
Above: A Silverson mising machine (courtesy Silverson Machines Ltd)

Musical instruments

R H Walker & Son Ltd came to Chesham in 1953 and started manufacturing and re-building organs at premises in Wey Lane. It was run by Peter R J Walker who came from a long line of organ builders going back to the 16th century. He learned his skills whilst being apprenticed to his father's business in Ruislip. Although they developed and made new organs, a large part of the company's work was in re-building and refurbishing existing instruments, for the life of an organ is normally 50 to 100 years. This typically meant renovating the old pipes, adding replacements where necessary and carrying out maintenance on the whole instrument. In the late 1950s Walker's developed a small organ with mechanical action called 'The Chesham' organ. It had one manual of five stops and the pedals permanently coupled. The company left Chesham around 1970.

Another specialist musical instrument, the bagpipe, was made in Bellingdon at the end of the century by **David Naill Co**, started by Les Cowell in 1976. Les re-located in 1989 to Somerset where the business is still thriving.

An R H Walker organ installed at All Saints Church, Chalfont St Peter

Pencils and pencil leads

In 1932 Mr R R Apel and his nephew Mr Lorenz Kress came to England and started a business in Wembley. Three years later they moved to Bellingdon Road, Chesham where they established the **Atlas Pencil Company.** Initially the business was to make leadslips for fitting into wooden pencils. All grades of lead were made with various compositions of graphite and clay. In 1941 the original building was practically burned to the ground but, because of the high proportion lof products exported, the Board of Trade gave great assistance to fund a temporary building which allowed the company to be back in full production within a few months.

After the war the building was completed and a test and development laboratory added.

One of the development team was Dr F Hardtmuth, who was a direct descendent of the man who helped to invent the method for making pencil leads. Soon the main business became the manufacture of leads for propelling pencils which were becoming increasingly popular. Leads were made in graphite, with colours for all the leading brands of propelling pencil. When Mr Apel died in 1949, Mr Kress took over as managing director and became a well known and respected figure in the Chesham business community. Business continued to grow and eventually, when a wood encasement department was added, complete pencils were made. Major contracts were won with government departments, educational authorities and cosmetic companies. The work force rose to 50 and an evening shift was introduced.

In the early 1960s the company joined forces with Joseph Egerton & Co Ltd who ran the Royal Ensign Pencil Works in Manchester. In 1965 the company sold a 49 percent share to Hardtmuth's and the remainder in 1972 when the Chesham factory was closed and all work transferred to a new facility in Bideford, North Devon.

Drawing of the rebuilt Atlas Pencil Co factory, Bellingdon Road

Atlas pencils and leads (courtesy Chesham Museum)

Miscellaneous products

A privately owned company that was founded in 1936, **Heat Efficiency Ltd,** has been based in Chesham since 1940. Whilst the business has involved design, maintenance and installation of heating systems, the company became well known for the development and manufacture of a scale solvent called **Kilrock**. Based in Church Street for many years, the company moved to Alma Road in the 1990s.

In 1955 Percy Lague and Arthur Dines started a company in Willesden called **Safety Service Co. Ltd.** They moved it to Chesham in the late 1960s and settled into the old Canada Works and renamed it Itex Works. Here they made and marketed industrial safety products for eye, face, head and mouth protection bearing the Itex trade mark. As business grew, they also moved into the old Empire Works in Station Road, later relocating to Asheridge Road and finally to Alma Road. At one time about 60 people were employed in the town but the business left Chesham in 1986 when it was sold to a company in Suffolk.

The Amersham Road site was then taken over by **Banaglaze Window Systems**, part of the Banfix Group of companies, manufacturers of replacement doors and windows. Conservatories have subsequently been added as an important part of the company's business which is now based at Crown Business Estate in Berkhampstead Road.

For nearly 30 years Chesham has been home to **B-Loony**, a leading manufacturer of promotional goods including balloons, sweatshirts, umbrellas, hats etc. Originally based in East Street the company moved to Springfield Road in 1984, then Higham Road, eventually settling in Bellingdon Road and Sunnyside Road *(pictured)*.

Durston Rolling Mills, a privately owned family business was founded in 1961 in Chalfont St Giles, but to accommodate continuing growth, settled in Hospital Hill, Chesham in 1993. Durston products are used throughout the world in a wide range of applications including gold and silversmithing, jewellery manufacture, wire shaping and flattening, material marking and patterning and numerous other areas where metal is required to be rolled. The business closed in Chesham in 2007.

This building in Sunnyside Road has at various times been called Sunnyside House, Chapel Works, Panel House and now Buck House

A line of small scale specialist rolling mills at Durston's

Chapter 15

War work

The Second World War, not surprisingly, had a huge impact on the town, not least on the factories and the remaining workforce. Some factories were taken over completely, whilst others were given instructions on what they were to make for the war effort. For security reasons much of this was not documented and today wartime work seems to have left little trace of its existence.

The arrival of Hivac and Modern Wheel Drive in the town and the takeover of Shillaker's Alma Road factory have already been described. The Co-operative Society also lost the use of its main function room at the Co-operative Hall, which became a British Restaurant, and its remaining staff who were not in the services were required to do essential services such as delivering milk and bread. The Co-op, despite receiving compensation from the Government, did not get its Hall back until well into 1947.

Anecdotal evidence from long-term Chesham residents indicates that the following war work also took place in the town:

Army boot manufacture

Barnes boot factory, Addison Road

Giffard Newton, Townsend Road

Dispensing and packing of glucose powder

Van Houten's, Temperance Hall, Church Street

Dispensing and packing of soap powder

near Barclays Bank, Broadway

Preparation and packing of egg powder

Bury Farm, Pednor Road

Preparation of 'M&B' labels

small room at the Co-operative Hall,
Upper High Street

Wooden spacer 'bomb' blocks

Thomas Wright's, Berkhampstead Road.

Aircraft parts manufacture

Empire Works, Station Road

Aircraft parts manufacture

Canada Works, Amersham Road

Hurricane propellers manufacture

behind Brandon's store, Broadway

Assembly of searchlights and torpedo generators

Arthur Lyons Co, in part of Amersham Woodware
and Toy Works, Moor Road

Wooden shovel manufacture

James East, Broad Street

Manufacture of Mosquito fuselage parts

Webb Jarratt, Townsend Road

Brush handles, tent poles

Sundt, Alexander Street

CHESHAM URBAN DISTRICT COUNCIL

British Restaurant

IS

NOW OPEN

TO ALL AT

THE CO-OPERATIVE HALL

HIGH STREET

to serve

Lunches from 12 noon to 2.30 p.m.

PRICES—

Soup and Bread - 3d.
Meat and Vegetables 8d.
Sweet - - - - 3d.
Tea or Beverage - 1d.

The Co-operative Hall, one of the buildings commissioned for the war effort (RE)

Postscript

As the 20th century came to an end, the industrial scene in Chesham was changing rapidly, reflecting the situation globally, but companies were still moving into the town as others closed or left. Most of the traditional industries are now gone; the last of the boot manufacturers has closed, the brewery finished almost half a century ago, one steadfast brush-making operation remains, and the timber yards and turners are much diminished. However, there are still many small, thriving businesses tucked away in the estates and yards, several involved in pharmaceuticals, information technology and engineering. Chesham remains a hive of industrious activity.

Many of the large, well-built Victorian factories in Waterside and Newtown were demolished as the industries that created them declined or moved away. At the same time, the Springfield and Asheridge Road industrial estates expanded their warehousing and light industrial units to cater for modern commercial needs. Along the way some attractive buildings have been lost; the 'Garden Factory' was built by George Williams in 1946 and later occupied by Van Houten and Alcan – it was demolished in 2007. The Carsberg factory, also built in Asheridge Road in 1946 was a beautiful art-deco building, demolished in 2008.

Chesham should be proud of its industrial heritage and it would be a pity if the grand, brick-built Victorian factories are all lost, leaving little

Carsberg's factory in Asheridge Road. Built 1946. Demolished 2008

Above: The 'Garden Factory' in Asheridge Road, built in 1946.
Below: Demolished 2007

trace of what has come before. It is pleasing that Chesham's last boot factory, Giffard Newton's of Townsend Road, has been rescued from redevelopment and put to use by Workaid, a company which recycles tools for the Third World. Recently it was disappointing to see the attractive old Gas Works building in Waterside demolished and replaced by residential flats. Perhaps the demand for affordable accommodation could be met by converting factories, such as the old Hayes boot factory in Waterside, into contemporary residential or office units.

Thankfully, since 2004, Chesham has had its own Museum which presents, most professionally, a record of the town's past rooted in craft and industry. This book represents the huge surge in interest in local and family history in the last decade and draws upon the substantial archive of photographic and written information now available to the public.

A modern view over Newtown to the industry of Asheridge Road (ABW)

Acknowledgements

John Armistead — JA
Dick Askew
Richard Barnes
Judy & Matthew Barr — JMB
Pauline Bates
Anna Beaven — ABE
Dora Beechey
Russell Barker — RB
Alan Bickerton
Albert Braithwaite — ABW
Alan Branigan — AB
Bill Brett
Alex Broad — ABR
Bob Bruton — BB
Edna Bunker
Robin Carsberg — RC
Laurie Craker — LC
Anne Crabbe — AC
Ann Daley
David Darvell
Cliff Davies
Janet Dineen
Brian Dunn — BD
Ray East — RE
Sheila Evans — SE
Lillian Ferguson
Madeleine Fletcher
Gill Glenister
Leslie Harborne — LH
Brian Harris
Janet Harris

(William) Rupert Hawes
Anthony Hawkins
David Heistercamp — DH
Chris Honey
Ron How
Bill Howard — BH
Brian Kay — BK
Stuart King — SK
Jason Kingdom
Peter Larkin — PL
Margaret Long — ML
Barrie Lucke
Brian Kay
John & Philip Mead — JPM
Patricia Miller — PM
John Munger
Gordon Nash — GN
Clive Newton — CN
Ben Nixon
Glyn Olden
Geoff Olney — GO
Stuart Ottley
Marjorie Pappin
John Pearson
Roger Perry
Bill Phillips
Bobbie Potter
Hilary Povey
A Puddephatt — AP
David Rance
Godfrey Reynolds

Keith Richardson
Len Riley — LR
Robert & Alan Russell — RAR
Chris Ryan
Colin Seabright — CS
Rodney Sedgewick — RS
Gwen Simmons
Nick Siney
Eddie Small — ES
Bill Studley
Bryan Wardle
Pete Webb
John West — JW
Janice Wilkinson
Peter Wright

Organisations which have helped with the use of photography

Royal Bucks Laundry basket
© the Buckinghamshire County Museum collections (pages 5 and 38)

Aerial view © English Heritage National Monuments Record Aerofilms Collection (pages 8 and 9)

Title page illustration courtesy of the Women's Institute (CS)

Sheffield Museum of Anaesthesia SMA

People's History Museum

Lucky Bears Ltd

Resources

We recommend the following publications, which have proved useful in researching Chesham's history

Baines, A. and Birch, C., *A Chesham Century*, 1994
Birch, C., *The Book of Chesham*, 1974
Birch, C. and Armistead, J., *Yesterday's Town: Chesham*, 1977
Hunt, J., *Chesham – A Pictorial History*, 1997
Patterson, G., *Chesham Between the Wars*, 2002
Piggin, G., *Tales of Old Chesham*, 1993
Piggin, G., *More Tales of Old Chesham*, 1995
Seabright, C., *Chesham in Old Picture Postcards*, 1-3, 1985-95
Seabright, C., *Chesham Yesterday & Today*, 1996
Seabright, C., *Images of England – Chesham*, 2004
Chesham & District Directory, 1914-1915
Chesham Town Talk magazine, 1994-2008

Kelly's Directory of Chesham & Amersham, 1847-1941
Tithe map and assessment, 1842
The Bucks Examiner, 1889-2008

We are also grateful to the following organisations for their research and archival material
Centre For Buckinghamshire Studies, Aylesbury
Local Study Centre, Chesham Library
Chesham Museum (www.cheshammuseum.org.uk)
The Chesham Society
The Francis Trust (Chesham Town Museum Project)

Further research on Chesham's boot and shoe making factories, with additional notes on the industry's centre at Northampton, and boot manufacture nationwide, has been carried out by John Pearson of Chesham, and is available to view at Chesham Museum.

This book would not have been possible without the archival work carried out by Ray East of Chesham over several decades. His photographic collection has provided many of the illustrations in this publication, for which the authors are extremely thankful.

Index of surnames